FamilyCircle

paintedfurniture

100+ Home Decorating Projects

FamilyCircle

painted furniture
100+ Home Decorating Projects

sixth&spring
books

Editorial Director
Trisha Malcolm

Art Director
Chi Ling Moy

Book Editor
Michelle Lo

Book Manager
Cara Beckerich

Copy Writers
Daryl Brower
Cathy Vail

Copy Editor
Pat Harste

President and Publisher, Sixth&Spring Books
Art Joinnides

Family Circle Magazine

Editor-in-Chief
Susan Kelliher Ungaro

Executive Editor
Barbara Winkler

Creative Director
Diane Lamphron

Assistant Editor
Robin Ruttle

How-to Editor
Peggy Greig

Library of Congress Cataloging-in-Publication Data
Painted furniture: 100+ home decorating projects / C Family circle;
[editor-in chief, Trisha Malcolm]
    p. cm.
    ISBN: 1-931543-30-5
    1. Furniture painting--Amateurs' manuals. 2. Interior
decoration--Amateurs' manuals. I. Malcolm, Trisha, 1960- II.
Family circle.

TT199.4.P32 2004
747--dc22   2003057340

Manufactured in China
1 3 5 7 9 10 8 6 4 2

First Edition

table of contents

introduction

One snowy Saturday morning when I was 10, my mother woke my sister, Bernadette, and me up with the news that we were going shopping. "Now," she explained, "I'm not talking grocery shopping. We're in search of a new bedroom set." I remember the excitement as we climbed into the car. This was going to change my life—a bed, a chest of drawers, and a desk (!) all my own. I also remember the disappointment. We headed to the fancy-shmancy furniture store downtown, where I beheld the bedroom set of my dreams: it was an absolute vision of flowers in bright bold hues—cascading wisteria, dancing daffodils, ravishing roses, all trellised around vines woven across a pale wood background. It was also way out of our price range. We left for a discount store, and as hard as I tried, I could not get the thought of that ensemble out of my head, especially when we ended up buying a gold-edged plain white set. I comforted myself with the fact that the desk opened into a vanity, and covered up the fact that my real fantasy wasn't fulfilled.

Or so I believed. Hiding disappointment from my mom was not as easy as I thought. The next morning on the way home from church, we took a detour to the art supply store. My brothers grumbled, wanting to get home to watch the game; my dad had that look on his face he always gets when he has a secret he's just bursting to tell; and my mom shooed me and Bernadette in and headed straight for the stencils. There, she let us choose cutouts of our favorite flowers—the blooms that eventually made their way across our simple bedroom set and wound their way into our dreams until we left for college.

Last summer, we presented this furniture to my 3-year-old twin nieces. Hannah and Emma reacted with the same joy and awe as my sister and I did when my mom—with some stencils, some paint, a little imagination and lots of heart—transformed that inexpensive plain white suite into a work of wonder.

That is what we set out to do in this book: To open your heart, your mind, to spark your imagination. We will show you how easy it is to fulfill your dreams—and the dreams of those you love. —Cathy Vail

easy flower pots, page 112

painting primer

Decorative painting used to be out of reach of most do-it-yourselfers, best left to custom-furnishing experts. Not any more! With the plethora of products and tools available--conveniently found at most craft and hardware stores—it's a cinch to create eye-catching effects and master myriad techniques. In general, most finishing processes fall into two categories: personalized decorative painting, and antiquing. But the line between these two classifications is frequently blurred, and both require the same basic set-up and tools. Before beginning your project, there are certain elements to take into consideration.

Getting Started

Create a clean and safe environment. Make sure that the room you are working in has adequate ventilation. A lot of the materials you'll be using— such as chemical strippers, glazes, varnishes, etc.—contain strong solvents. Wear a mask and rubber gloves. Use a drop cloth to protect surfaces. Keep cotton rags or a roll of paper towels nearby to clean up any spills as soon as they occur.

Have all the necessary supplies at hand. Each project requires unique items to create your desired effect, but all call for a number of specific tools. Clean, well-maintained brushes are foremost; the type you choose depends on what kind of paint you are using. Synthetic brushes (most often nylon) are great for water-based latex and acrylic paints. If you are working with oils, opt for the more expensive natural-bristle brushes—it will be worth the few extra bucks. Sable-hair brushes are key to the success of small projects and for detail work and touch-ups. Sponge brushes are inexpensive and give you an immaculate, streak-free finish, but they wear out quickly. (I used them on a Mondrian-inspired sideboard I painted, as they were great for the detailed edges, but replacing them after virtually every use ended up costing me a small fortune.) Medium- and fine-grade sandpaper is integral (a sanding block will also help out), as well as a steel wool. Pick up plenty of stir sticks and rolls of masking tape (in varying widths).

flower-trimmed dresser, page 40

Budget your time. Patience is paramount. Whether you're waiting for the piece to dry after stripping or between coats, don't rush it. The beauty of your finished project is dependent upon respecting the time it takes to complete each interim step.

Practice makes perfect. If you're new at this, try out your techniques before embarking on your undertaking. This is especially important when working with several layers of color, or trying to copy a particular effect such as marbling.

Selecting your paint. Oils are the traditional choice for decorative painting. But with their excessive drying time, they're both a blessing and a curse. On the one hand, they give you more time to work and to correct any mistakes you make, but they're frustratingly slow to dry, which means having to allow much more time in between steps. The cleanup is also daunting; it's time-consuming and the chemicals are extremely toxic.

Water-based latex and acrylic paints are much easier to deal with. They dry faster, which is a major advantage when you are applying several coats of paint; cleanup is effortless; and they're environmentally friendly. They do have a lower margin of error in terms of fudging goofs, though, so be sure that you meticulously plan out your project before you begin.

Another alternative is to employ a combination of the two. If you use a nonporous water-based paint for priming and base coating (it has to be satin, semigloss or gloss to be nonporous), you can still work with an oil-based paint or glaze. (Important: Don't use water-based products on top of oils—they will bead.)

As with all techniques, the final appearance depends on your choice of base and finishing colors.

Preparing to Paint

Every project has individual requirements that must be followed to get the surface ready for painting. You may be starting out with a pristine piece of unfinished furniture, or you may be bringing a flea market find back to life. To guarantee that your piece ends up looking as beautiful as you imagined it, carefully follow all the steps.

Cleaning. Paint can't bond to a surface unless it's clean and porous. Make sure all surfaces are free of stains, grease, dirt, wax and dust. Tack cloths are also good to wipe surface of all dust. Remove hardware, knobs, hinges, etc. For unpainted furniture, use a mild detergent or soap to clean the surfaces, then rinse well—very well. For previously painted, varnished or stained wood, use wood cleaner, mineral spirits or wax remover. Wait for the piece to dry for at least a day before proceeding to the next step—though the wood may feel dry on the surface, it's probably still damp underneath. Painting before the piece is dry leads to bubbles.

Stripping. With used furniture, you don't have to worry about stripping unless it's in really bad shape—it peels, flakes or has multiple layers of paint or varnish. If that's the case, then treat the piece with a chemical stripper. For horizontal surfaces, such as a tabletop, a liquid stripper is suggested; for vertical and more elaborate woodwork, apply a gel or paste stripper. Follow the manufacturer's instructions, but be patient and let the chemicals do the work! (The paint is ready to remove when your scraper glides effortlessly across the surface, lifting up a layer of "sludge," revealing the clean base below.) Using a scraper or putty knife, take off the old layers, being careful not to gouge the wood. Steel wool or an old toothbrush (dipping them in stripper will up their effectiveness) takes care of hard-to-reach areas. After you have removed as much of the finish as possible, clean the stripper from the wood, following the manufacturer's instructions. Again, allow the piece to thoroughly dry before you embark on the next step--sanding.

Sanding. All wood--new, newly stripped or previously painted—has to be sanded before it can be primed. But before sanding, fill in any dents or holes with wood filler or putty. Let dry. Then, using a sanding block and going with the grain of the wood, keep sanding (yes, it's tedious) until you have a smooth surface. With painted furniture, sand the old paint lightly so it will be porous enough to accept the primer. Change the

white-washed cupboard, page 28

animal-print boxes, page 106

sandpaper frequently. For curves and recessed molding areas, double up a sheet of sandpaper to get into nooks and crannies.

Priming. Priming seals the wood, enabling it to evenly take on color. Previously painted pieces need to be primed to avoid peeling and chipping. Primers are water-, oil-, or alcohol-based (Note: If you use an oil-based primer, you will have to use oil paints in your project). Shellac, an alcohol-based primer, is one of the best sealers for unpainted wood. It goes on smoothly, requires less sanding, and is quick-drying. Apply the first coat of primer; once it is completely dry, sand until smooth. Apply a second coat, dry, and then sand again before applying your base coat. The base coat you use depends on the decorative or antiquing technique you will be employing.

Decorative Effects

Now is the time to reap the results of all that hard work! There are several fantastic finishes to choose from: sponging, faux painting, stenciling, striping, and découpaging. Get ready to release your

imagination—and start creating.

Sponging. This is one of the simplest—and most evocative—techniques. The application of several colors gives way to effects ranging from subtle to spectacular. The result depends on the hues you choose for your base coat and sponging colors. Tones from the same color family yield a rich sophisticated finish. Contrasting colors, such as sponging dark or brilliant hues over a pale base, can be overpowering and is therefore not suitable for large projects. Limit your color selection to four or less. Sponging is a great camouflaging method—perfect for pieces whose surfaces are not in the best condition. For delicate patterning use a sea sponge; household cellulose sponges account for a more rugged-looking surface. Because sponging is accomplished quickly, opt for fast-drying latex or acrylic paint.

Faux painting. With its decidedly modern feel, faux painting is versatile, dramatic and easy to achieve—after a little practice. The object in faux finishing is to make something look like something it's not. Faux marble, stone and animal prints are among the most popular techniques.

Marbling. The exquisite nature of marble is deceptively simple to replicate, bringing a touch of class to any project. Use this technique sparingly, on smaller pieces or as an accent. When deciding on hues, go with Mother Nature--cool grays, cloudy blues, earthy greens, and pale yellows. Before you begin marbling, make sketches of your desired effect, so you'll feel confident when it comes to the real thing. Consult photographs of real marbling; they will reveal the nuances that make this a successful technique. If you're a novice, use a feather to achieve your veining pattern; it will yield light, varied strokes. More experienced painters can use a fine round pointed brush for an equally deft touch. Vary the tone of each vein, giving it its own character. Veins should not cross and should be unevenly spaced and not parallel to one another. Change the pressure you apply on the feather or brush to produce different widths. Veins should be asymmetrical; they should "shiver" across the surface, like fine cracks.

Granite. Stone is similar to marbling in that it lends itself to improvisation. Look at photos of granite before getting started. When selecting your colors, make sure the base coat is one shade darker than your topcoat. While the topcoat is still wet, wad up plastic wrap and blot it onto the paint, exposing the base coat. Dip a sea sponge that has been torn into small pieces into your next color. Blot onto a paper plate to remove excess paint; lightly press over the entire surface. The paint should look uneven. Continue sponging on (use a different sponge for each color) chosen hues until desired effect is reached. Use a maximum of six additional colors.

Animal prints. Go on a safari! Animal prints are all the rage. Refer to an animal print on an item of clothing or in a book to pick your pattern. After applying the base, either draw the shapes in with a pencil or paint them freehand. Zebra stripes, leopard spots and tortoise shell work particularly well. Stencils are also available in a variety of prints and will make your hunting go a little easier.

Stenciling. You don't have to be an accomplished artist to master stenciling. The tools accessible today—copy machines to duplicate a

apothecary cabinets, page 116

design, transparent acetate sheets to facilitate the painting and a wide variety of store-bought pre-cut stencils—make it a breeze to put your signature on any project. Designs can be as simple or as complex as you want. Stencil over any base coat, using acrylics or oils. A shorthaired brush or stenciling crayon will give you a fine finish with defined edges. Use a light hand and apply as little paint as possible to guard against bleeding under the stencil. Work in soft circular strokes or a light dabbing motion, slowly building up color. Keep a separate brush available for each color.

Striping. This is one of the most attractive ways to give a simple piece major pizzazz. Whether broad or narrow, stripes equal attitude--take a page from a buttoned-down pinstriped suit or embrace the jaunty jubilance of beach awnings. (Note: Stripes highlight irregularities; your surface must be smooth.) Masking tape is key to this finish—plan the width of your stripes and then position the stripes. Paint over the tape, using long strokes so the paint doesn't seep under the edges. Leave to dry—this is imperative! Carefully peel tape with a smooth movement to reveal the clearly delineated lines beneath. 3M now offers a flatback masking tape to give super sharp print lines on smooth surfaces. Follow manufacturer's directions for use.

Découpaging. Like stenciling, découpage gives you freedom to transfer images that lend whimsy and originality to an item. Follow the individual instructions about each project. Almost any image—from magazines, postcards, photos, etc.—is suitable for this technique, and will shout out, quietly or vociferously, who you are. Spray adhesive or découpage medium keeps the image in place, though you must apply the medium sparingly so the surface doesn't bubble. For an heirloom ambiance, use this technique on distressed or antiqued pieces.

Antiquing

Antiquing gives an artfully aged appearance to furniture. Whether you are distressing a spanking new unpainted piece or weathering a flea-market treasure with crackle medium, antiquing lends sophistication and charm.

Quite often a project will employ antiquing as well as one of the above decorative painting finishes--success is guaranteed when all the steps are carefully followed.

Glazes account for antiquing's signature look. Though they're sometimes used in decorative painting, translucent glazes add depth and dignity to the surface and are the not-so-secret ingredient in antiquing. How you apply the glaze and manipulate it when it's still damp is what defines the individual techniques. Ready-mixed glazes can be found in paint or art supply stores--as with all paints, water-based acrylic glazes are easier to use and cleanup is simple, oil-based glazes lend a richer finish, allow you more time to work, but are extremely difficult to clean.

Crackling. This finish reproduces the look of old, weathered paint, adding "instant" heritage to any piece. A thick coat of crackle glaze produces large cracks; finer cracks are achieved with a thin coat. Apply your base coat—this is the color that will show through the cracks. Then apply the crackle medium using long, smooth, even strokes. Don't brush back and forth—apply in one direction only. Allow glaze to dry (usually about 4 hours, but check manufacturer's instructions). Apply topcoat evenly in the same direction that you applied the crackle—again, don't brush back and forth. The cracks will appear soon after application.

Distressing. This classic antiquing technique, which gives wood a distinctive aged appeal, can be achieved in one of two ways, scarring or cloth distressing. Scarring works best when you start out with an unpainted piece that is going to be finished using one of the decorative painting techniques described above. Take a rubber hammer and dent the corners and top of the furniture you are distressing. A length of chain or a set of keys dragged across the top also does the trick. Wormholes can be copied by heating a nail or other pointy object until it is red hot, then driving it into the wood with a hammer. Keep the holes small and close together (study the formation of real woodworm holes before attempting this).

Cloth distressing is usually a finish in itself, not paired with another technique. The process "distresses" the piece by using rags (cotton or linen is ideal) to apply a thin glaze. Depending on what you are distressing, you will probably need more than one rag—stick with the same material throughout to keep the texture consistent. Apply glaze directly on top of your base coat. Dip a 2-foot-square rag into the glaze and wring out. Bunch rag, tucking in ends, creating multiple ridges. Use a deft touch when applying, rearranging the rag often to create myriad patterns. The variations in tones of your imprints give it the authentic distressed look. This is a process that benefits from practice runs.

Finishing Up

Now that your masterpiece is complete, how are you going to seal and protect the surface? Varnish is the transparent layer that makes your finish fool-proof and can also add a dimension of depth—dark colors recede while the lights pop. Apply varnish only when your piece has completely dried--err on the side of caution. Oil varnish should be thinned with paint thinner and shouldn't be used over light finishes because it tends to yellow. Oil polyurethane is great over freehand painting, preventing peeling. Acrylic varnish can only be used over water-based paints, but dries fast and has minimal yellowing; the same is true with water-based polyurethane. Shellac is also a good sealer, but it's extremely difficult to use as a final coat and requires an expert touch. Whichever varnish you choose, apply several thin coats using even strokes and lightly sanding with wet sandpaper between coats. All varnishes are available in a number of finishes, from matte to high gloss; make sure you choose the right one to enhance your project.

Store it with style. Cabinets, hutches and trunks all provide the perfect canvas for painted pleasures.

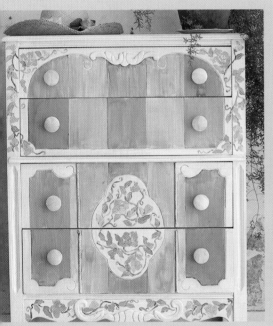

holding patterns

dressers, armoires and cabinets

What a difference a little paint makes! A coat of creamy white and a few carefully placed painted apples turn a battered cabinet into a charming country accent. Stencils make it ultra easy to duplicate the design.

You need: Wooden hutch and wooden knobs; all-purpose primer; indoor/outdoor acrylic paint in cream; acrylic craft paint in burnt orange, brown, red and green; stencils to fit hutch: basket of apples, single apple and triple apples; stencil adhesive; waterbased satin finish varnish; screwdriver; #120 and #220 sandpapers; tack cloth; 1"/2.5cm and 2"/5cm flat paintbrushes; ½"/1.3cm flat artist's brush; ½"/1.3cm and 1"/2.5cm stencil brushes; ruler; cellophane tape; paper plates; paper towels.

Preparing surface: Remove knobs, drawers, doors and hardware; set hardware aside. Sand all surfaces to be painted (including side and back edges of drawers) using #120, then #220 sandpapers. Wipe clean with tack cloth. Apply two coats of primer following label directions. Let dry thoroughly. Sand with #220 sandpaper. Wipe clean with tack cloth.

Painting: Use 2"/5cm brush for large areas and 1"/2.5cm brush for small areas. Apply two to three coats of cream to each piece, including knobs, allowing each coat to dry thoroughly before applying the next coat. For best results, lightly sand between coats using #220 sandpaper and wipe clean with tack cloth; do not sand after last coat. Let dry overnight. Using ½"/1.3cm flat brush, paint top outer edge burnt orange. Let dry overnight.

Weathering: Using #220 sandpaper, sand random areas down to raw wood. Wipe clean with tack cloth.

Stenciling: Refer to stenciling how-tos on page 11. On basket stencil, mask off all design elements around basket with tape. Spray wrong side of stencil with adhesive. Adhere stencil to door front. Using 1"/2.5cm stencil brush, stencil basket burnt orange. Carefully lift up stencil and position on second door. Clean stencil before repositioning to prevent smudges. Stencil second basket in the same manner. When paint is dry, re-adhere stencil to first door, lining up stencil over stenciled basket. Using ½"/1.3cm stencil brush, shade outer edges and handles of basket brown, as shown. Repeat for second door. Remove tape, then wash and dry stencil. Wash brushes; let dry.

Mask off all design elements around apples with tape. Spray wrong side of stencil with adhesive again if necessary. Adhere stencil to door, lining up stencil over stenciled basket. Using 1"/2.5cm brush, stencil apples red. Repeat for second door. Remove tape, then wash and dry stencil. Wash brush; let dry. Working in the same manner, stencil leaves green using 1"/2.5cm brush and then stems brown using ½"/1.3cm brush. Wash brushes; let dry.

Working as before, stencil two single apples on each drawer front and two triple apples to backboard, as shown. Let dry overnight.

Finishing: Apply two coats of varnish to all surfaces, allowing each coat to dry before applying next coat. Let dry 24 hours before using.

Assembling: Install hardware and rehang doors. Install knobs, then slide in drawers.

stenciled apple hutch

You need: Unfinished pine cupboard with dowel insert doors and wooden knobs; Minwax Accents semi-transparent stain in rustic orange and hunter green; Minwax Pastels stain in slate blue; Minwax Fast-Drying Polyurethane in satin finish; screwdriver; #120 and #220 sandpapers; tack cloth; rubber gloves; old tee shirts; scissors; 1"/2.5cm flat natural bristle paintbrush; blue painter's tape.

Preparing surface: Remove drawers, doors and knobs; set hardware aside. Sand all surfaces to be stained (including back edges of drawer) using #120, then #220 sandpapers. Wipe clean with tack cloth.

Staining: Work in a well ventilated area and wear rubber gloves and old clothes. Cut tee shirts into 6"/15.2cm squares. For inside of cupboard, all sides of drawer (except front and back edges of front) and knobs, apply slate blue using a clean cloth. Allow stain to penetrate for up to one minute. Wipe off excess with a dry clean cloth. Additional coats may be applied for a deeper color. Allow to dry at least four hours between coats. After staining is completed, let dry 24 hours.

Apply painter's tape along edges of doors near dowels to protect them from rustic orange stain. For outside of cupboard and dowels, apply rustic orange using a clean cloth. Apply first coat in direction of wood grain, working quickly to obtain coverage. Let stain penetrate 2-6 minutes, then wipe any excess with a clean cloth. Be sure to wipe in the direction of the grain, while blending light and dark areas to obtain uniform color. Remove tape. Tape dowels near door frame to protect from stains. Repeat to stain door frames and front of door with hunter green. Remove tape.

Finishing: Using brush, apply one to two coats of polyurethane to all pieces, allowing each coat to dry before applying next coat. Let dry 24 hours before using.

Assembling: Rehang doors, install knobs, then slide in drawer.

TIP

Any uneven color penetration can be blended, if done immediately. Work a liberal amount of stain into the surface and rub lightly to blend color. To deepen color, apply additional coats. Allow to dry about four hours between coats.

See-through washes of colored wood stain lend a quaint look to a plain pine sideboard.
A simple fixer-up, this folksy orange cupboard is accented with a hunter green trim.
Detailed doors with dowels add an airy touch.

rustic cupboard

You need: Wooden armoire with recessed panel doors and wooden knobs; all-purpose primer; indoor/outdoor acrylic paint in red and light blue; waterbased satin finish varnish; screwdriver; #120 and #220 sandpapers; tack cloth; 1"/2.5cm flat paintbrush; ½"/1.3cm flat artist's brush; blue painter's tape; pencil; ruler; scissors.

Preparing surface: Remove knobs, doors and hardware; set knobs and hardware aside. Sand all sides of armoire and doors using #120, then #220 sandpapers. Wipe clean with tack cloth. Apply one to two coats of primer following label directions. Let dry thoroughly. Sand with #220 sandpaper. Wipe clean with tack cloth.

Painting: Apply two to three coats of paint to each piece, allowing each coat to dry thoroughly before applying the next coat. Use 1"/2.5cm brush for large areas and ½"/1.3cm brush for tight areas and for any needed touch-ups. For best results, lightly sand between coats using #220 sandpaper and wipe clean with tack cloth; do not sand after last coat.

Paint outside of armoire red and inside light blue. Paint wrong side of doors and outer edges red. On right side of each door, paint entire inside panel light blue. For stripes, measure inside width of panel, then divide the number by three; this is the stripe width. On inside of panel, measure and mark for width of center stripe. Adhere two strips of painter's tape down entire length of inside panel, having one long edge of tape butting marks. Paint center stripe and frame red. Let dry four hours. Remove tape then continue to let dry overnight. Erase pencil marks.

Finishing: Apply two coats of varnish to all pieces, including knobs, allowing each coat to dry before applying next coat. Let dry 24 hours before using.

Assembling: Install hardware, hang doors, then install knobs.

TACK CLOTHS

A tack cloth is a sticky piece of fabric that is often used to remove dust after sanding. Though they can be purchased at a local hardware store, they can be made just as easily. Thoroughly soak a cotton rag or piece of cheesecloth in spoiled shellac, rosin or something tacky. Squeeze out the excess, and voila!

Gain some extra closet space (and a fun spot to store clothes) with an unfinished armoire jazzed up with sassy stripes. Keep the colors bold and bright for extra impact and finish with whimsical door pulls.

striped armoire

Lend a luxe look to a plain cabinet by topping it with a faux tortoise finishing and washing the front and sides with layers of complementary paint tones. Tables, boxes and trunks also take beautifully to this technique.

Note: The techniques used here are ragging and color washing.

You need: Wooden sideboard with wooden knobs; all-purpose primer; indoor/outdoor acrylic paint in bone; acrylic craft paint in mustard, rust and brown; glazing medium for acrylic craft paint; small paint bucket; waterbased satin finish varnish; #120 and #220 sandpapers; tack cloth; 2"/5cm and ½"/1.3cm flat paintbrushes; paper plates; small paint bucket; cotton rags such as cut up tee shirts; blue painter's tape.

Preparing surface: Remove doors, latch and knobs; set hardware aside. Sand all surfaces to be painted using #120, then #220 sandpapers. Wipe clean with tack cloth. Apply one to two coats of primer following label directions. Let dry thoroughly. Sand with #220 sandpaper. Wipe clean with tack cloth.

Painting: Using 2"/5cm brush, apply two to three coats of paint to each piece, allowing each coat to dry thoroughly before applying the next coat. For best results, lightly sand between coats using #220 sandpaper and wipe clean with tack cloth; do not sand after last coat. Paint top mustard. Paint latch, knobs and rest of sideboard bone. Let dry overnight.

Ragging top: Dampen two rags. Pour small amounts of rust and brown onto separate paper plates. Crumple rags and dip one into each color. Blot onto surface. Turn and move rags to avoid making repeat patterns. Overlap colors, applying rust on top of brown and brown on top of rust, while allowing base coat to show through in areas as shown. Let dry overnight.

Color washing: Dampen a rag. In bucket mix one part bone with three parts glazing medium. To

this add ⅛ parts each of mustard and brown. Working a section at a time, brush on mixture, then wipe with rag, using long strokes, from top to bottom. Color wash doors and rest of sideboard. Let dry overnight.

Door panel detail: Apply tape to either side of door panels' recesses. On paper plate mix one part mustard with one part glazing medium. Using 1/2"/1.3cm brush, paint panel recesses. Let dry 2 hours and remove tape. Let dry overnight.

Door panels: Apply tape to edges of panels to mask off recesses.

Dampen two rags. Pour one part mustard and one part brown onto separate paper plates. To each add two parts glazing medium. Crumple rags and dip one into each color. Blot mustard onto door panels. While still wet, blot on brown. Let dry 2 hours and remove tape. Let dry overnight.

Finishing: Using 2"/5cm flat brush, apply two coats of varnish to all pieces, allowing each coat to dry before applying next coat. Let dry 24 hours before using.

Assembling: Install hardware, rehang doors, then install knobs and latch.

elegant sideboard

You need: Wooden bureau with wooden knobs; all-purpose primer; indoor/outdoor acrylic paint in beige and light gray; acrylic craft paint in black, medium gray, ochre and burnt sienna; glazing medium for acrylic craft paint; small plastic cups; small paint bucket; waterbased satin finish varnish; screwdriver; #120 and #220 sandpapers; tack cloth; 2"/5cm flat paintbrush; ½"/1.3cm flat; ⅛"/.3cm wide flat artist's brush; #1 and #6 artist's round brushes; blue painter's tape; large sea sponge.

Preparing surface: Remove drawers from bureau and remove knobs from drawers. Sand all surfaces to be painted (including side and back edges of drawers) and knobs using #120, then #220 sandpapers. Wipe clean with tack cloth. Using 2"/5cm brush, apply two coats of primer following label directions. Let dry thoroughly. Sand with #220 sandpaper. Wipe clean with tack cloth.

Painting: Use 2"/5cm brush for large areas and ½"/1.3cm brush for tight areas and for any needed touch-ups. Apply two to three coats of paint to each piece, allowing each coat to dry thoroughly before applying the next coat. For best results, lightly sand between coats using #220 sandpaper and wipe clean with tack cloth; do not sand after last coat. Paint knobs black. Paint top, sides and bottom front skirt of frame light gray. Paint front of frame ochre. Paint drawer fronts, including side and back edges, beige. Let dry overnight.

Tiger maple details: To make glaze, mix one part burnt sienna paint with ½ part glazing medium in a cup. Use ⅛"/.3cm wide flat brush to make vertical strokes across horizontal drawer frames as shown. Use #1 round brush to make patches of repetitive strokes, overlapping the patches down the vertical drawer frames. Let dry overnight. Apply tape where tiger maple areas are adjacent to light gray paint.

Sponging off: To make glaze, mix one part medium gray paint

with four parts glazing medium in a bucket. Working a section at a time and using 2"/5cm brush, brush on mixture then lightly blot area using a dampened sponge. Turn and move sponge to avoid making repeat patterns. Immediately glaze and sponge adjacent areas to avoid hard edges. Rinse sponge as needed. Let dry two hours; remove tape. Continue to let dry overnight.

Finishing: Using 2"/5cm flat brush, apply two coats of varnish, allowing each coat to dry before applying next coat. Let dry 24 hours before using.

Assembling: Install knobs, slide in drawers.

An old chest of drawers can easily double as a dining room sideboard. We gave this low-lying piece a Far East finish by using faux painting techniques to create a tiger maple front. The top, sides and drawers are painted in contrasting shades.

tiger maple bureau

Get graphic by covering an unfinished dresser with a basecoat of white and topping it with a grid of yellow. A ruler and a steady hand are all it takes to recreate this totally mod look; doing it is fast, fun and fabulous.

You need: Wooden dresser; all-purpose primer; indoor/outdoor acrylic paint in white and pale blue; acrylic craft paint in yellow; waterbased satin finish varnish; #220 sandpaper; tack cloth; 1"/2.5cm flat paintbrush; artist's brushes: #4 round and ½"/1.3cm flat; ruler; measuring tape; pencil; blue painter's tape; paper plate.

Preparing surface: Remove drawers from dresser and apply primer in the same direction as wood grain. Leave to dry. Apply white paint to all surfaces and, when dry, sand slightly. Wipe with tack cloth and apply second coat of paint; leave to dry. Replace drawers and mark out design in pencil. Working outwards so that design is even, draw 4"/10cm –wide vertical bands, spacing them 5"/12.5cm apart. Mask outside of bands and paint in pale blue. Remove tape immediately, pulling it back on itself as close to surface as possible, and leave paint to dry. Repeat to create horizontal bands. To create fine yellow lines, draw a line ½"/1.3cm from all edges of the blue bands. Dilute green paint with a little water. Using round brush, paint along each pencil line and leave to dry.

Finishing: Remove drawers and apply two coats of varnish, allowing to dry after each coat. Replace drawers.

A CLEAN EDGE

To get a razor straight edge, try supporting your hand with a mini bean bag—it will help keep your hand steady and make it easier to achieve straight lines. Painter's tape, which removes easily and cleanly, also works wonders. We recommend 3M's Scotch Safe-Release Painter's Masking Tape for Faux and Decorative Painting.

tiled dresser

The timeworn look of this small-scale cabinet is easily achieved with a resist technique using rubber cement. Coat the painted cabinet with finishing wax, then buff to a soft sheen that will infuse it with an instant patina.

You need: Wooden cupboard with wooden knob; all-purpose primer; indoor/outdoor acrylic paint in light yellow and pale gray; waterbased satin finish varnish; screwdriver; #120 and #220 sandpapers; tack cloth; 1"/2.5cm flat paintbrush; ½"/1.3mm flat artist's brush; rubber cement; paint scraper; finishing wax; soft cloth.

Preparing surface: Remove door and knobs; set hardware aside. Sand all surfaces to be painted using #120, then #220 sandpapers. Wipe clean with tack cloth. Apply one to two coats of primer following label directions. Let dry thoroughly. Sand with #220 sandpaper. Wipe clean with tack cloth.

Painting: Using 1"/2.5cm brush for large areas and ½"/1.3cm brush for tight areas, apply two to three coats of yellow to all surfaces, allowing each coat to dry before applying next coat. For best results, lightly sand between coats using #220 sandpaper and wipe clean with tack cloth; do not sand after last coat. Let dry overnight.

Weathering effect: Apply thin strokes of rubber cement across all flat surfaces (including knob) and thicker patches around areas of natural wear and tear, such as edges. Let dry. Apply one coat of gray; let dry four hours. To remove rubber cement, use edge of paint scraper to lift up edge of rubber cement, then carefully peel off. Continue to let dry overnight. Sand using #220 sandpaper to soften edges of weathering effect. Wipe clean with tack cloth.

Finishing: Apply a liberal coat of finishing wax to all pieces. Buff to a soft sheen using soft cloth.

Assembling: Rehang door, then install knob.

TIP

For a more spirited look, try using starkly contrasting colors such as a bright red base coat with a turquoise top coat or a hunter green base coat with a chalky yellow top coat for a dramatic effect.

white-washed cupboard

Bring out the molding details on a 'vintage' piece in a cool autumn palette, then découpage the top with motifs cut from wine-label gift wrap. Once done, apply a color photocopy of grapes from a botanical print to the door.

You need: Wooden cabinet with wooden knobs; all-purpose primer; matte-finish latex paint in cranberry, cream and green; pine-finish waterbased wood stain; waterbased satin finish varnish; #120 and #220 sandpapers; tack cloth; 1"/2.5cm and 3"/7.6cm flat paintbrushes; ¼"/.6cm and ½"/1.3cm flat artist's brushes; pencil; ruler; blue painter's tape; wine label printed gift wrap; color photocopy of botanical grape image to fit door; découpage medium; scissors; soft cloth for stain.

Preparing surface: Remove door, drawers and knobs; set hardware aside. Sand all surfaces to be painted using #120, then #220 sandpapers. Wipe clean with tack cloth. Apply one to two coats of primer following label directions. Let dry thoroughly. Sand with #220 sandpaper. Wipe clean with tack cloth.

Painting: Use 1"/2.5cm brush to apply two coats of cream paint to drawer fronts and inside panel of door; let dry. Apply two coats of cranberry paint to inside and outside of cabinet; let dry. Apply tape to drawer fronts, exposing ¾"/2cm border; paint border green. Remove tape; let dry. Apply tape to drawer fronts, exposing ¼"/.6cm band around green border; paint band cranberry. Remove tape; let dry. Apply tape to edges of inside panel of door; paint outer edge green. Remove tape; let dry. Paint knobs green. When all paint is dry, sand all edges with #220 sandpaper. Replace door and knobs.

Découpaging: Cut rectangle of gift wrap 1"/2.5cm smaller all around than top of chest. Cut rectangle into geometric shapes, keeping pieces in order. Starting at one corner, coat backs of pieces with medium and press onto top, smoothing outward to eliminate air bubbles; let dry. Cut out grape photocopy; apply to front of door in same way.

Staining: Use cloth to wipe all surfaces with satin. Let dry overnight.

Finishing: Use 3"/7.6cm brush to apply two coats of varnish to all pieces, allowing each piece to dry before applying next coat. Let dry 24 hours before using.

Assembling: Install hardware, rehang door, then install knobs and slide in drawer.

divine wine chest

You need: Wooden armoire with recessed panel doors and wooden knobs; all-purpose primer; indoor/outdoor acrylic paint in light gray and medium brown; acrylic craft paint in gray-green, burnt orange and white; glazing medium for acrylic craft paint; waterbased satin finish varnish; stencils to fit armoire doors: multiple part poppy stencil set, and small, medium and large ferns; stencil adhesive; #120 and #220 sandpapers; tack cloth; screwdriver; 3"/7.6cm flat paintbrush; 1"/2.5cm flat paintbrush; 1"/2.5cm stencil brush; ruler; paper plates; paper towels; small paint bucket; cheese cloth.

Preparing surface: Remove knobs, doors and hardware; set hardware aside. Sand all surfaces to be painted using #120, then #220 sandpapers. Wipe clean with tack cloth. Apply one to two coats of primer following label directions. Let dry thoroughly. Sand with #220 sandpaper. Wipe clean with tack cloth.

Painting: Use 3"/7.6cm brush for large areas and 1"/2.5cm brush for tight areas and for any needed touch-ups. Apply two to three coats of light gray, allowing each coat to dry thoroughly before applying the next coat. For best results, lightly sand between coats using #220 sandpaper and wipe clean with tack cloth; do not sand after last coat. Let dry overnight.

Stenciling: Refer to stenciling how-tos on page 11 and to poppy stencil set directions. Spray wrong side of flower center stencil with adhesive. Adhere stencil to one door front, as shown. Using stencil brush, stencil centers burnt orange. Carefully lift up stencil and position on second door. Stencil centers in the same manner. Wash brush; let dry.

Spray wrong side of first petal stencil with adhesive. Adhere stencil to one door front, lining up stencil over stenciled centers. Mixing white with burnt orange, stencil petals various shades of light burnt orange. Working in the same manner, repeat for other door and for second petal stencil. Wash brush; let dry. Working in the same manner, stencil some stems and leaves gray-green, then others a lighter shade by mixing in white. Wash brush; let dry. Refer to photo for suggested placement of ferns. Spray wrong side of each stencil with adhesive. Stencil small fern first, medium second and large third, allowing each to dry before proceeding to the next size. Stencil small and medium ferns gray-green mixed with white, and large fern gray-green. Clean stencil before repositioning to prevent smudges. Stencil bottom left panel first. Clean adhesive from back of large stencil, turn stencil over to reverse the image and spray back of stencil before stenciling top right panel. When all stenciling is completed, let dry 24 hours.

Ragging off: To make glaze, mix one part brown paint with four parts glazing medium in bucket. Working a section at a time and using 3"/7.6cm brush, brush on mixture then lightly blot area using dampened cheese cloth. Turn and move cloth to avoid making repeat patterns. Immediately glaze and rag off adjacent areas to avoid hard edges. Allow glaze to remain along edges of recessed panels. Replace cheese cloth as needed. Let dry overnight.

Finishing: Using 3"/7.6cm brush, apply two coats of varnish to all pieces, allowing each coat to dry before applying next coat. Let dry 24 hours before using.

Assembling: Install hardware, rehang doors, then install knobs.

Floral stencils create a romantic look on the doors of an old-fashioned armoire. The technique is easy to master and wonderfully low maintenance.

fern and poppy armoire

Bring some unexpected color into the kitchen with this bold country hutch. Slick a solid hue over an unfinished or timeworn piece, then use stencils to paint on farmyard fowl.

You need: Wooden hutch with glass doors and wooden knobs; all-purpose primer; indoor/outdoor acrylic paint in lilac and golden yellow for outside and a slightly lighter shade for inside; acrylic glass paint in orange, red, yellow and black; waterbased satin finish varnish; screwdriver; #120 and #220 sandpapers; tack cloth; 2"/5cm flat paintbrush; artist's brushes: #3 and #6 round and ½"/1.3cm flat; chicken and chick stencil; 1"/2.5cm stencil brush; stencil adhesive; blue painter's tape; paper plates; paper towels.

Painting: Remove glass doors and knobs. Following painting tips, sand and prime hutch. Paint hutch with lilac paint. If desired, paint inside of hutch with a lighter shade of paint to counteract the shadows and lighten inside spaces. Paint knobs with golden yellow paint. Add details to knobs with fine paintbrushes and colors as desired.

Stenciling: Place glass doors on a flat, well protected surface for ease in stenciling. Spray both sides of stencils with adhesive to help keep from slipping while working on project. Position chicken stencil on glass and tape in place. Dip stencil brush in paint and remove excess on paper towels. Working with small amount of paint on stencil brush, pounce it up and down to stencil design. Stencil chickens with orange paint. Let dry before adding details. Clean stencils before repositioning them. Turn chicken stencils over where motifs face in opposite direction. Again turning stencils as needed, stencil combs with red and spots with green. Stencil chicks with yellow. If desired, stencil designs on both sides of glass, lining up motifs so design is reversed. Add details with artist's paintbrushes.

Finishing: Apply two coats of varnish to all pieces, allowing each coat to dry before applying next coat. Let dry 24 hours before using.

Assembling: Install hardware, rehang doors, then install knobs.

TIP

When stenciling with more than one color, always start with the lightest shades and work your way to the darker tones. And, always use one brush for each color to minimize the risk of accidental "muddiness."

farmyard kitchen hutch

Stenciling is a simple and easy way to dress up any plain old piece of furniture. Transform a basic chest into an attractive work of art by painting decorative ivy and roses along one side.

You need: Wooden chest with wooden knobs; all-purpose primer; indoor/outdoor acrylic paint in ivory; acrylic craft paint in dark rose and dark green; ivy and roses garland stencil (size to fit your chest) and single rose stencil; stencil adhesive; waterbased satin finish varnish; #120 and #220 sandpapers; tack cloth; 1"/2.5cm flat paintbrush; 1¼"/.6cm and ½"/1.3cm stencil brushes; ruler; pencil; blue painter's tape; cellophane tape; scissors; paper plates; paper towels.

Preparing surface: Remove drawers and knobs. Sand all surfaces to be painted (including side and back edges of drawers) using #120, then #220 sandpapers. Wipe clean with tack cloth. Apply one to two coats of primer following label directions. Let dry thoroughly. Sand with #220 sandpaper. Wipe clean with tack cloth.

Painting: Apply two to three coats of ivory to drawers, knobs and chest, allowing each coat to dry before applying next coat. For best results, lightly sand between coats using #220 sandpaper and wipe clean with tack cloth; do not sand after last coat. Let dry overnight. Slide in drawers.

Stenciling: Refer to stenciling how-tos on page 11. Position stencil on left front of chest drawers so leftmost rose is at least ¼"/.6cm from side edge of drawers. Apply a vertical strip of painter's tape that butts right side edge of stencil, then apply another strip that continues to bottom edge of chest, then one that continues to top and back edge of chest. Measure to make sure strip is straight; make adjustments if necessary. Trim off top and bottom edge of stencil to within ⅜"/1cm of design elements. Mask off all design elements around roses with cellophane tape. Spray wrong side of stencil with adhesive. Adhere stencil to upper front of chest, lining up right side edge of stencil with painter's tape. Using ¼"/.6cm stencil brush, stencil roses with dark rose. Carefully lift up stencil and position for next repeat below. Clean stencil before repositioning to prevent smudges. Repeat to bottom of chest. On top of chest, work from the front edge to back. Remove cellophane tape from stencil, then wash and dry stencil. Mask off all roses with cellophane tape. Spray wrong side of stencil with adhesive again if necessary. Adhere stencil to upper front of chest, lining up stencil over stenciled roses. Using ½"/1.3cm stencil brush, stencil leaves dark green. Continue to work in the same order. Wash brushes; let dry.

Working in the same manner, stencil single rose to right front corner of chest top as shown, using ½"/1.3cm stencil brush for rose and ¼"/.6cm stencil brush for leaves. Let dry overnight.

Finishing: Remove drawers. Apply two coats of varnish to all pieces, allowing each coat to dry before applying next coat. Let dry 24 hours before using.

Assembling: Install knobs, then slide in drawers.

chest with
stenciled roses

Tiny tweeters perched atop watermelon slices lend a lovely, lighthearted note to a pine cabinet. Paint the bird and fruit designs and cover the remainder with a distressed finish. Paint the panels in bright hues, then add in the motifs.

You need: Wooden cupboard with raised panel door, wooden knob and latch; all-purpose primer; acrylic paint in yellow and blue; acrylic craft paint in aqua, black, white, dark pink and green; waterbased satin finish varnish; screwdriver; #120 and #220 sandpapers; tack cloth; 1"/2.5cm flat paintbrush; artist's brushes: ⅛"/.3cm, ¼"/.6cm and ½"/1.3cm flat, #1 and #3 round; graphite paper; pencil; tracing paper.

Using paintbrushes: Use 1"/2.5cm brush for large areas and ½"/1.3cm flat artist's brush for edges.

Using artist's brushes: Choose the appropriate size brush for the area or detail to be painted. Use flat brushes for painting straight lines and round brushes for birds, beaks, melon flesh and seeds. To make bird's eyes, use end of paintbrush handle to apply a dot of paint.

Preparing surface: Remove knob, latch, door and hardware; set hardware aside. Sand all surfaces to be painted using #120, then #220 sandpapers. Wipe clean with tack cloth. Apply one coat of primer following label directions. Let dry thoroughly. Sand with #220 sandpaper. Wipe clean with tack cloth.

Painting: Apply two coats of yellow to entire cupboard, both inside and out, allowing each coat to dry before applying next coat. For best results, lightly sand between coats using #220 sandpaper and wipe clean with tack cloth; do not sand after second coat. Without sanding between coats, paint as follows: paint raised door panels, knob and latch aqua. Paint all but raised panels blue. Let dry overnight.

Weathering: Use #220 sandpaper to sand random areas down to yellow paint. Wipe clean with tack cloth.

Decorative painting: Enlarge pattern for bird on a photo copier so it measures 5⅛"/12.8cm from beak to tail. Enlarge pattern for watermelon so it measures 9⅛"/23cm across top edge. Copy bird onto tracing paper. Turn tracing over and use as pattern for bottom bird. Using graphite paper, transfer designs to door, as shown. Referring to photo for color placement, paint light colors first, then dark. Mix colors together to make more shades. Add details like eyes and seeds last. Let dry overnight.

Finishing: Apply two coats of varnish, allowing each coat to dry before applying next coat. Let dry 24 hours before using.

Assembling: Install hardware. Rehang door.

folk art jam cupboard

You'll need: Wooden dresser with wooden knobs; all-purpose primer; indoor/outdoor acrylic paint in off white; Plaid Decorator Glazes™ in sunflower, ivy green, new leaf green, vibrant pink and pale violet; Plaid Decorator Blocks™ Sweet Pea; waterbased satin finish varnish; screwdriver; #120 and #220 sandpapers; tack cloth; 1"/2.5cm and 2"/5cm flat paint brushes; #00 and #4 round artist's brushes; ruler; pencil; blue painter's tape; paper plates; paper towels.

Preparing surface: Remove knobs and drawers. Sand all surfaces to be painted (including side and back edges of drawers) using #120, then #220 sandpapers. Wipe clean with tack cloth. Apply two coats of primer following label directions. Let dry thoroughly. Sand with #220 sandpaper. Wipe clean with tack cloth.

Painting: Using 2"/5cm brush, apply two to three coats of off white to each piece, allowing each coat to dry thoroughly before applying the next coat. For best results, lightly sand between coats using #220 sandpaper and wipe clean with tack cloth; do not sand after last coat. Let dry overnight. Replace drawers.

Marking: Referring to photo, use pencil to lightly outline the areas to be glazed in sunflower. Use ruler for any straight lines. Remove drawers.

Sunflower glazing: Use 1"/2.5cm brush to apply sunflower glaze to top, sides, outlined areas of front, including drawers, and feet. Let dry overnight. Erase pencil marks. Marking glazed stripes: Replace drawers. Referring to photo, mark for stripes. Remove drawers.

Glazing stripes: Use tape to mask around outside and center stripes. Use 1"/2.5cm brush to apply ivy green glaze. Let dry 2 hours and remove tape. Let dry overnight. Mask around two light green stripes and apply new leaf green glaze. Let dry 2 hours and remove tape. Let dry overnight. Replace drawers.

Glazing feet: Use 1"/2.5cm brush to apply new leaf green to top half of feet. Use #4 artist's brush to paint banding using ivy green glaze.

Using Decorator Blocks: Using a separate plate for each color, squeeze glaze onto paper plate. Use 1"/2.5cm brush to apply a small amount of glaze to detailed surface of block. Use all fingers to press block firmly onto surface. Do not allow block to slip or design will smear. Lift block straight off surface. To use a different color using the same block, clean block by pressing it onto paper towels.

Flowers and foliage: Print sweet pea flowers and buds in vibrant pink and pale violet. Make some leaves ivy green and the rest new leaf green. See photos for suggested arrangements. Paint stems and tendrils using #00 artist's brush.

Finishing: Use 2"/5cm brush to apply two coats of varnish to all surfaces, allowing each coat to dry before applying next coat. Let dry 24 hours before using.

Assembling: Install knobs, then slide in drawers.

Even a beginner can detail a once-drab chest of drawers with romantic blossoms. The design is actually stamped on with decorator blocks; tone-on-tone stripes provide the perfect backdrop.

flower-trimmed dresser

Have a piece in need of a facelift? Marry old-style charm with modern sensibility by freshening a flea-market find with a coat of paint and a great geometric design. Dressers, pie safes and cupboards are all potential makeover candidates.

You need: Wooden cabinet; all-purpose primer; indoor/outdoor acrylic paint in light blue; acrylic craft paint in white and dark blue; waterbase satin finish varnish; screwdriver; #120 and #220 sandpapers; tack cloth; ½"/1.3cm and 2"/5cm flat paint brushes; #0 round artist's brush; double-sided tape; 8½" x 11"/21.6cm x 27.9 cm typing paper; pencil; pencil compass; ruler; scissors.

Preparing surface: Remove door and hardware; set hardware aside. Sand all surfaces to be painted (including side and back edges of drawers) using #120, then #220 sandpapers. Wipe clean with tack cloth. Apply two coats of primer following label directions. Let dry thoroughly. Sand with #220 sandpaper. Wipe clean with tack cloth.

Painting: Using 2"/5cm brush, apply two to three coats of light blue, allowing each coat to dry thoroughly before applying the next coat. For best results, lightly sand between coats using #220 sandpaper and wipe clean with tack cloth; do not sand after last coat. Let dry overnight.

Making patterns: Using compass and ruler, draw circles with the following diameters on typing paper as follows, marking each with appropriate letter: Make seven 1"/2.5cm circles (A), six 1⁷⁄₁₆"/3.6cm circles (B), 12 1⁹⁄₁₆"/3.9cm circles (C), five 1¹³⁄₁₆"/4.5cm circles (D), four 2"/5cm circles (E), three 2¼"/5.7cm circles (F), two 3"/7.6cm circles (G), one 3¹³⁄₁₆"/9.6cm circle (H) and one 4¼"/10.5cm circle (I). Cut out circles.

Positioning circles: Apply double-sided tape to back of each circle. Referring to diagram for placement, apply circles to door panels, adjusting position and spacing for your size door. For concentric circles, tape smaller circle to larger, matching holes made by compass point.

Painting: Use compass point to make a tiny hole into door panel through hole in circle. Remove paper and draw circle into wood. Repeat for all sizes. For concentric circles, use same hole in panel to draw both circles. Paint outlines of circles using pointed brush, then fill in using flat brush. Refer to photos for colors. Apply one to two coats as needed.

Finishing: Using 2"/5cm brush, apply two coats of varnish to all surfaces, allowing each coat to dry before applying next coat. Let dry 24 hours before using.

Assembling: Install hardware and rehang door.

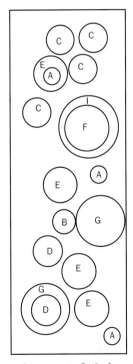
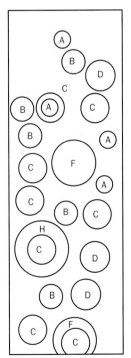

Placement of Circles

bathroom keeper

You need: Wooden jelly cabinet with wooden knob; all-purpose primer; indoor/ outdoor acrylic paint in dark blue; acrylic craft paint in cream and brick red; waterbased satin finish varnish; #120 and #220 sandpapers; tack cloth; 2"/5cm flat paintbrush; artist's brushes: ⅛"/.3cm, ¼"/.6cm and ½"/1.3cm flat and #3 round; pencil; ruler; carpenter's level; blue painter's tape; paper plate.

Preparing surface: Remove door and knob; set hardware aside. Sand all surfaces to be painted using #120, then #220 sandpapers. Wipe clean with tack cloth. Apply one to two coats of primer following label directions. Let dry thoroughly. Sand with #220 sandpaper. Wipe clean with tack cloth.

Marking cabinet: Using pencil, ruler and level, mark 9"/23cm diagonal squares on side and door

of cabinet, as shown. Draw an evenly spaced diagonal grid in each square. Mark 3"/7.6cm diagonal squares along upper edge of cabinet. Adjust sizes of squares, if needed, to match size of cabinet.

Painting: (Note: Paint the inside of cabinet. Raw wood does not wear well.) Apply tape along edge of each square, placing tape within outline. Using 2"/5cm brush, apply two to three coats of dark blue to all surfaces, except squares, allowing each coat to dry thoroughly before applying the next coat. For best results, lightly sand between coats using #220 sandpaper and wipe clean with tack cloth; do not sand after last coat. Let dry 2 hours and remove tape. Let dry overnight.

Painting dots: Dip end of an artist's brush into cream paint and touch to surface to make a dot.

Make groups of three dots randomly over blue paint. Let dry overnight.

Squares: Apply tape outside each square. On paper plate, mix 1 part cream with one-quarter part red to make light red. Mix 1 part cream with one-quarter part dark blue to make light blue. Referring to photo for suggested motifs and using the artist's

brushes, paint each square to resemble a quilt square. Let dry 2 hours and remove tape. Let dry overnight.

Finishing: Using 2"/5cm flat brush, apply two coats of varnish to all pieces, allowing each coat to dry before applying next coat. Let dry 24 hours before using.

Assembling: Install hardware, rehang doors, then install knobs.

Blanket a seen-better-days cabinet or an unfinished pine piece in a graphic quilt motif. Tiny flowers painted over a dark background echo the look of country calico; top with patchwork squares arranged in traditional diamond design.

calico jelly cabinet

*Sponge it, stamp it; spray it, stencil it—
homebound pieces take to paint beautifully.*

fabulous furniture

tables, chairs and more

You need: Wooden coffee table with drawers and wooden knobs; paper map; all-purpose primer; indoor/outdoor acrylic paint in pale yellow; FolkArt acrylic craft paints in wicker white, Amish blue, camel and buttercup; waterbased satin finish varnish; #120 and #220 sandpapers; tack cloth; sea sponge; paper plates; 1"/2.5cm flat paint brush; artist's brushes: ⅛"/.3cm, ¼"/.6cm and ½"/1.3cm flat, #1 and #3 round; ruler; pencil; for optional stenciling: alphabet stencil, ½"/1.3cm stencil brush and stencil adhesive; screwdriver; cellophane tape; graphite paper.

Using paint brushes: Use 1"/2.5cm brush for large areas and ½"/1.3cm flat artist's brush for edges.

Preparing surface: Remove drawers and knobs. Sand all surfaces to be painted (including side and back edges of drawers) using #120, then #220 sandpapers. Wipe clean with tack cloth. Apply one to two coats of primer following label directions. Let dry thoroughly. Sand with #220 sandpaper. Wipe clean with tack cloth.

Painting: Using 1"/2.5cm brush for large areas and ½"/1.3cm brush for tight areas, apply two to three coats of pale yellow to all surfaces, allowing each coat to dry before applying next coat. For best results, lightly sand between coats using #220 sandpaper and wipe clean with tack cloth; do not sand after last coat. Let dry overnight.

Making map pattern: Enlarge map, in sections, on a photo copier to fit table top; as shown. Tape sections together.

Painting map: Paint elements one at a time, allowing each color to dry before applying next color, or when still wet to blend colors. Apply two coats of wicker white to entire table top. Using pencil, mark off areas for label and compass. Thin Amish blue with water to make a wash. Using damp sponge, sponge over surface omitting marked off areas. Transfer design using graphite paper. Using paint thinned with water, paint island(s) camel, then outline and highlight (while paint is still wet) using a more concentrated color and also with buttercup. Paint label and compass buttercup, thinning paint with a little water. Paint or stencil lettering (see stenciling how-tos on page 11) using Amish blue. Paint decorative lines around perimeter with a darker concentrated shade of Amish blue. To give an aged effect, make a very thin wash with camel and sponge over some areas, as shown. Let dry overnight.

Finishing: Apply two coats of varnish to all pieces, allowing each coat to dry before applying next coat. Let dry 24 hours before using.

Assembling: Install knobs, then slide in drawers.

WASHING

The technique of washing is an easy way to create a mottled topcoat of paint. First, paint your project with your chosen basecoat. Then, dilute your topcoat color with water until the paint is the consistency of milk. Use the diluted paint to "wash" over the basecoat, working somewhat unevenly so the basecoat will show through. You can paint a wash with a sponge, a rag, or a brush. Just remember to spread the paint in different directions, building up more paint in some areas and less in others.

Travel the world from your living room. Make a pattern from a map enlarged to fit the surface you wish to cover, then letter by hand or with a purchased stencil. We chose a two-drawer coffee table for this project, but a trunk side table or any other flat-surfaced object will serve the same purpose.

map coffee table

Pens, papers, remote controls, game pieces and other odds and ends are attractively contained in this wooden catchall. A checkerboard stencil and art stamps create the folksy design; make it even more whimsical by adding a fish drawer pull.

You need: Wooden box with drawer; wooden fish-shaped drawer pull; all-purpose primer; acrylic craft paints in red, green, black and yellow; waterbased satin finish varnish; #220 sandpaper; tack cloth; ½"/1.3cm flat artist's brush; white candle; medium-grade steel wool; 1"/2.5cm stencil brush; checkerboard stencil to fit width of box; blue painter's tape; black ink stamp pad; small spiral and alphabet stamps; screwdriver.

Preparing surface: Remove drawer pull. Sand box; wipe with tack cloth.

Painting: Paint box with primer, then two coats of red paint; let dry.

Distressing: Rub candle over sections of caddy and drawer. Apply two coats of green paint; let dry. Rub caddy gently with steel wool to remove paint over waxed areas.

Stenciling: Tape stencil on caddy. Using stencil brush, pounce red paint on stencil. Remove stencil; let dry. Paint yellow outlines around squares. Stamp the word "fish" inside red squares with alphabet stamps; stamp spirals on ends of checkerboard. Paint edges of caddy black.

Finishing: Apply three coats of varnish, letting dry after each coat. Install fish-shaped drawer pull.

DISTRESSING

Distressing lends a soft and aged look to any piece of furniture. If you are looking to create a more dramatic effect, employ high contrast colors such as a blue base color and yellow top coat. Applying more wax, which will result in a greater "see-thru" effect, will also lend greater textural interest. If a more authentic age is what you want, gauge and scrape off areas of the piece with a small tool such as a utility knife or chisel. Do this mainly on corners and edges.

country-days caddy

You need: Wooden storage bench; all-purpose primer; acrylic paints in red, dark brown and black; waterbased satin finish varnish; wood putty; small putty knife; #220 sandpaper; tack cloth; 1"/2.5cm flat paint brush; ½"/1.3cm flat artist's brush; sea sponge; combing tool; paper towels; clean flannel rags.

Preparing bench: Sand bench; apply two coats of primer, letting dry after each coat.

Painting: Apply two coats of red paint, letting dry after each coat.

Preparing glaze: Mix two parts dark-brown paint with one part black; thin with water to make glaze.

Glazing: Dip sponge in glaze; blot on paper towels to remove excess. Starting at back of bench, lightly pounce glaze onto arms, legs and bottom spindle panel; let dry.

Combing: Lightly brush glaze onto one spindle; "comb" with tool from top to bottom. Comb remaining spindles in same way. Apply thin coat of glaze to bench seat; using rag, rub glaze off in spots for weathered look. Repeat applying and rubbing off glaze to achieve desired look. Let dry overnight.

Finishing: Apply three coats of varnish, letting dry after each coat.

COMBING

When using the combing technique you should generally choose a stronger, darker color for the bottom coat and a lighter, more neutral shade for the top. Although both colors will show, the topcoat usually slightly hides or leaves a somewhat translucent film over some of the areas of the bottom coat.

A mix of clever sponging, ragging, combing and staining gives an unfinished pine bench the look of antiqued wood. The finished result is an expensive looking piece perfect for placement in an entryway or hall.

splendid storage bench

Little details go a long way. Topped with bold black spirals and a wavy background (created by pulling a comb through still-wet glaze) an unassuming occasional table becomes a room-defining focal point.

You need: Wooden oval table; all-purpose primer; indoor/outdoor acrylic paint in black; acrylic craft paint in medium brown and ochre; small tube artist's watercolor in burnt sienna; shellac; white vinegar; waterbased satin finish varnish; #120 and #220 sandpapers; tack cloth; 1"/2.5cm flat paint brush; 1"/2.5cm disposable sponge brush; #1 round artist's brush; paper plate; 6" x 2"/15.2cm x 5.1cm rectangle of matboard; craft knife; paper towels; tracing paper; pencil; white graphite paper.

Preparing surface: Sand using #120, then #220 sandpapers. Wipe clean with tack cloth. Omitting table top, use flat brush to apply one to two coats of primer following label directions. Use sponge brush to apply one coat of shellac to table top. Let dry thoroughly. Sand all surfaces with #220 sandpaper. Wipe clean with tack cloth.

Painting: Using flat brush, apply two to three coats of black to table skirt and legs, allowing each coat to dry before applying the next coat. For best results, lightly sand between coats using #220 sandpaper and wipe clean with tack cloth; do not sand after last coat. Apply two to three coats of medium brown to table rim. Let dry overnight.

Combing: On a paper plate, mix ochre with ½ part water. Use flat brush to apply one coat of mixture to table top. Let dry one hour.

To make combing tool, cut ½"/1.3cm wide notches with ¼"/.6cm wide teeth in long edge of matboard. To make glaze, thoroughly mix burnt sienna watercolor on a paper plate with ⅙ part vinegar. Use flat brush to apply one coat of glaze to table top. While wet, comb surface in a wave pattern as shown. Wipe away drips on table rim as they occur. Let dry overnight

Accent painting: Trace patterns onto tracing paper. Trace nine spirals and four "S" curves. Arrange on table top as shown. Do not tape. Combed surface is easily scratched so proceed with care. Slip graphite paper underneath a pattern and go over lines to transfer. Remove tracings. Paint black using round brush. Let dry overnight.

Finishing: Apply two coats of varnish to all surfaces, allowing each coat to dry before applying next coat. Let dry 24 hours before using.

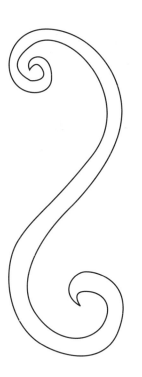

oval table

You need: Wooden adirondack chair, ottoman and table; all-purpose primer; indoor/outdoor acrylic paint in bright orange and hot pink; #120 and #220 sandpapers; tack cloth; 1"/2.5cm flat paint brush; ½"/1.3cm flat artist's brush; blue painter's tape.

Preparing surface: Sand all surfaces, including undersides, using #120, then #220 sandpapers. Wipe clean with tack cloth. Apply one to two coats of primer to all surfaces following label directions. Let dry thoroughly. Sand with #220 sandpaper. Wipe clean with tack cloth.

Painting: Referring to photo for color placement, apply two to three coats of bright orange, allowing each coat to dry before applying next coat. For best results, lightly sand between coats using #220 sandpaper and wipe clean with tack cloth; do not sand after last coat. Let dry overnight.

Apply painter's tape to all edges where hot pink will meet bright orange. Apply two to three coats of hot pink, allowing each coat to dry before applying next coat. Use ½"/1.3cm flat brush to get into tight areas and for any needed touch-ups. Sand between coats same as before. Let dry two hours and remove tape. Continue to let dry 24 hours before using.

TIP

The key to a lasting paint job is starting with a clean, well-prepared surface. For small jobs, use a soft bristle brush with a mild soapy solution to remove all debris. A mild bleach solution can be used to kill any mold and mildew growing on the surface. Use a spray water bottle to apply the solution; rinse off with plain water.

For tougher or bigger projects, you may want to use a power washer, which can be rented at most paint stores for a minimal fee. Take special care to read all the safety instructions before operating the machine—the high-pressure water can cause damage if not used properly.

Color your world. A few quick strokes of high-voltage color turn a traditional Adirondack chair and ottoman into a show-stopping piece for poolside or patio. Add a matching side table for maximum impact.

adirondack set

You need: Straight-sided wooden coffee table or end table; all-purpose primer; acrylic craft paint in off-white and black; waterbased satin finish varnish; #120 and #220 sandpapers; tack cloth; 1"/2.5cm flat paint brush; 12" x 18"/30.5cm x 45.7cm sheets of Scratch Art Wax-O Stencil Paper; cellophane tape; ruler; fine-tip black permanent marker; cutting mat; craft knife; stencil adhesive; 1"/2.5cm stencil brush; paper plate; paper towels.

Preparing surface: Sand all surfaces using #120, then #220 sandpapers. Wipe clean with tack cloth. Apply one to two coats of primer following label directions.

Let dry thoroughly. Sand with #220 sandpaper. Wipe clean with tack cloth.

Painting: Apply two to three coats of off-white to all surfaces, allowing each coat to dry before applying next coat. For best results, lightly sand between coats using #220 sandpaper and wipe clean with tack cloth; do not sand after last coat. Let dry overnight.

Cutting stencil: Enlarge pattern on a photo copier to fit table as shown. To accommodate size of design, you will have to make a separate copy of each section, then tape together. Tape stencil paper to design. Trace outlines using marker. Working on cutting

mat, cut out sections using craft knife.

Stenciling: Refer to stenciling how-tos on page 11. Spray wrong side of stencil with adhesive. Adhere stencil to table top, then extend down sides and legs. Cut stencil to fit around legs as needed. Stencil using black. Let dry overnight.

Finishing: Apply two coats of varnish, allowing each coat to dry before applying next coat. Let dry 24 hours before using.

STENCIL TRICK

An option to using stencil adhesive to keep stencils in place is plain old masking tape. To ensure that the tape doesn't peel off any extra tackiness by applying it to your shirt and then peeling it off, before using for the stencil.

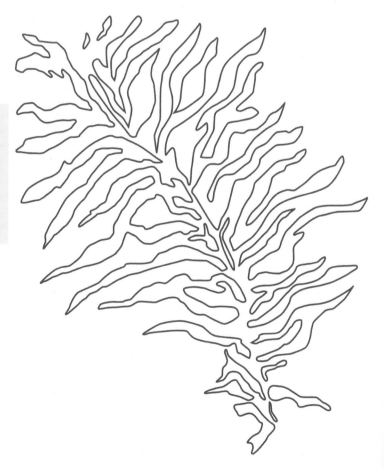

Animal prints never go out of style and this zebra painted Parson's table proves it. Paint with an off-white base coat, then stencil on the stripes for an eye-catching conversation piece perfect for a den or family room.

zebra side table

Cool, crisp and very contemporary: wide bands of color paint a winning pattern against white wicker. Masking tape is the key to the scheme, creating nice clean lines. Finish off with a cotton-covered cushion in a coordinating floral.

You need: Wicker chair; acrylic paints in white and light blue; wide, flat paint brush; 3"/7.5cm-wide masking tape; matte-finish spray varnish; feather duster; #120 and #220 sandpapers; tack cloth; blue floral-print cotton fabric; matching thread; blue cording to match fabric; 3"/7.5cm thick foam pad, cut to size of chair seat; sewing machine with zipper foot; sewing needle; pins; scissors; pencil; ruler.

Preparing surface: Dust chair to remove any pieces of paint or wood slivers within weave. Sand rough surfaces using #120, then #220 sandpapers. Wipe clean with tack cloth.

Painting chair: Apply several coats of white paint to entire chair, letting dry after each coat. Cover arm and seat trim with tape to protect from paint. Apply tape strips, 3"/7.5cm apart, across back,

sides and seat of chair. Apply two or more coats of blue paint to areas between tape strips, letting dry after each coat; remove tape. Apply two coats of varnish to entire chair, letting dry between coats.

Cutting fabric for cushion: Measure length and width of foam; add 1"/2.5cm to each measurement. Cut two pieces of fabric to these measurements for top and bottom of cushion. Add twice length to twice width, then add 1"/2.5cm; cut 4"/10cm-wide strip of fabric to this length for boxing strip.

Note: All stitching is done in ½"/1.3cm seams, with right sides facing and raw edges even, unless noted.

Sewing cushion: Pin cording to each long edge of boxing strip, placing base of cording ½"/1.3cm from raw edges of fabric. Using zipper foot, stitch cording to

boxing strip. Fold boxing strip in half crosswise; pin and stitch short ends together to form tube. Pin and stitch cushion top to one edge of boxing strip, placing boxing strip seam at center back edge and pivoting stitching at corners. Pin and stitch cushion bottom to other edge of boxing strip in same way, leaving back edge open. Insert foam; slip-stitch opening closed.

striped chair and cushion

POLKA DOT CHAIRS

You need for each: Wooden toddler size chair; Rust-Oleum Painter's Touch aerosol primer in white; Rust-Oleum Painter's Touch aerosol paint in a light and dark color such as: #1924 Country Blue and #1948 Spa Blue, #1951 Pretty Pink and #1950 Berry Bright, or #1952 Peach Delight and #1953 Real Orange; #120 and #220 sandpapers; tack cloth; old sheets or drop cloths; 2"/5cm-wide blue painter's tape; pencil compass; ruler; scissors.

Preparing surface: Sand all surfaces, using #120, then #220 sandpapers. Wipe clean with tack cloth. To prime, work in a well ventilated area. Place chair on sheet or drop cloth, then protect surrounding area to prevent over-spray. Following label directions, apply one coat of primer to all surfaces of chair, allowing each section to dry before proceeding to the next section. Let dry thoroughly.

Painting: Working as for priming, apply two coats of lighter color following application tips and drying times on label. Let dry overnight.

Working one polka dot at a time, use pencil compass to draw a 1"/2.5cm-diameter circle on painter's tape. Cut out, then adhere to chair; refer to photo for suggested placement. Continue until desired polka dot pattern has been achieved. Working as before, apply two coats of darker color. Let dry overnight; remove tape circles.

STRIPED FLOWER POTS

You need: Three clay pots and matching saucers to fit on your chairs; all-purpose primer; acrylic craft paint in colors shown or as desired; waterbased gloss finish varnish; ¼"/.6cm and ½"/1.3cm flat artist's brushes; pencil; books and magazines.

Priming: Using ½"/1.3cm brush, apply one to two coats of primer to all sides of pot and saucer following label directions. Let dry thoroughly.

Dividing for stripes: On work surface, stack as many books and magazines as necessary to achieve height of top edge of bottom stripe. Hold pencil flat on top of stack, then place pot on work surface so it touches pencil point. Holding pencil firm, rotate pot to draw a straight horizontal line around pot. Continue to work in this manner until you have desired number of guidelines for stripes.

Painting: Apply two to three coats of paint to all sides allowing each coat to dry thoroughly before applying next coat, using ¼"/.6cm brush for narrow stripes and ½"/1.3cm brush for wide stripes. Paint light stripes first, then dark stripes. Paint saucers. After all painting is completed, let dry overnight.

Finishing: Apply two coats of varnish, allowing each coat to dry before applying next coat. Let dry 24 hours before using.

Kid-size chairs make adorable places to set potted plants or bouquets of fresh cut flowers. Paint in cheerful sherbet shades and enhance with lighter toned dots. Terra cotta pots get a similar sprucing up when done in coordinating stripes.

polka dot chairs and striped flower pots

A fresh coat of paint and a few carefully placed stencils give a playroom-perfect facelift to a wood table and stools. Use S-hooks and a towel bar to store bags of game pieces, markers or crayons.

Note: See patterns on page 66 and 67.

You need: 30"/76.2cm-square wood table, 29"/ 73.7cm high; four 12"/30.5cm-square wood stools, 18"/45.7cm high; 24 wood pieces in desired shape and size (for game tokens); #120 and #220 sandpapers; tack cloth; all-purpose primer; acrylic paint in white, green (for number 1), yellow-green (for number 2), blue-green (for number 3) and light green (for number 4); water-based satin finish varnish; ¼"/.6cm and 1"/2.5cm flat paintbrushes; #00 round artist's brush; ⅜"/1cm stencil brush; ⅞"/2.2cm numbers stencil; stencil adhesive; white typing paper; glue stick; cellophane tape; graphite paper; metal-edged ruler; ballpoint pen; blue painter's tape; paper towels; paper plates; 24"/61cm-long chrome towel rack with screws; screwdriver; four 4"/10.2cm-long chrome "S" hooks; four dice (one for each player); ¾yd/.75m of 42"/106.5cm-wide dark ecru linen; matching sewing thread; scissors; straight pins; sewing machine; iron.

Preparing surface: Sand all surfaces to be painted using #120, then #220 sandpapers. Wipe clean with tack cloth. Apply one to two coats of primer following label directions. Let dry thoroughly. Sand with #220 sandpaper. Wipe clean with tack cloth.

Preparing: Cut apart numbers in pattern A (keeping measurement line with number 4) and glue each to center of typing paper. Enlarge patterns A and B on a photocopier. (Note: Pattern B is size of tabletop and will have to be photocopied in sections. Tape sections together.) Sand table, stools and game tokens first with medium, then with fine-grain sandpaper. Wipe with tack cloth to remove sanding dust.

(Continued on page 66)

game table set

(Continued from page 65)

Painting stools: Using 1"/2.5cm flat brush, apply two coats white paint. Let dry two hours after each coat. Tape numbers to center of stools. Slip graphite paper under photocopy and go over lines with ballpoint pen to transfer. Use a ruler to make straight lines whenever possible. Remove numbers. Paint numbers using assigned color. (Note: For easier painting, apply painter's tape to any straight lines.) Outline using pointed brush and fill in with ¼"/.6cm flat brush. Apply one to two coats as needed. Let dry overnight.

Finishing: Using 1"/2.5cm flat brush, apply two coats of varnish, allowing each coat to dry before applying next coat. Let dry 24 hours before using.

Painting table: Paint table white same as for stools. Tape pattern B to tabletop. Transfer pattern same as for stools. Do not transfer numbers inside horizontal bars—they will be stenciled. Referring to photo for color placement, paint numbers, circles and horizontal bars same as for stools. Let dry overnight.

Stenciling: Refer to pattern B for position and order of numbers.

Use tape to mask off numbers around number to be stenciled. Spray wrong side of stencil with adhesive. Position stencil on horizontal bar and adhere in place. Pour small amount of white paint on paper plate. To stencil, dip stencil brush in paint. Using a circular motion, work paint into brush on a pad of paper towels until brush is almost dry. Using same circular motion, lightly work over edge of stencil and onto table. Lift up stencil, then let dry 15 minutes. Clean stencil before repositioning to prevent smudges. Continue to work in this manner

until all numbers are completed. Let dry overnight. Varnish as for stools. Secure towel rack to center of one side, as shown.

Painting game tokens: Paint six game tokens in each of the four colors. Apply two coats of paint. Let dry. Apply two coats of varnish to all tokens.

Making token bags: To make four bags, cut sixteen 6" x 9"/15.2cm x 22.9cm rectangles (bags and lining) and four 2" x 6"/5.1cm x 15.2cm strips (hanging loops) of desired fabric. For each, fold hanging loop in half lengthwise, wrong sides facing;

pattern A

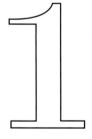

5"/12.7cm

press. Turn long edges ⅜"/1cm to inside; press. Sew together along length, ¼"/.6cm from edge. Set aside.With right sides facing, pin two rectangles together for each bag. Using ½"/1.3cm seam allowance, stitch around three sides leaving one short edge open. Press side seams open. Turn top edge ½"/1.3cm to wrong side and sew ¼"/.6cm from top edge; press. Turn top edge an additional 2"/5.1cm to wrong side and press. Topstitch around bag over previous stitching. Turn to right side.

Make linings same as for bags, but do not turn right side out. Slip lining inside bag, matching side seams and top edges; pin. Fold hanging loop in half lengthwise and insert 1"/2.5cm of ends between bag and lining, centered on one side; pin. Sew around top of bag, ¼"/.6cm from top edge. Hang bags from towel rack with "S" hooks.

pattern B

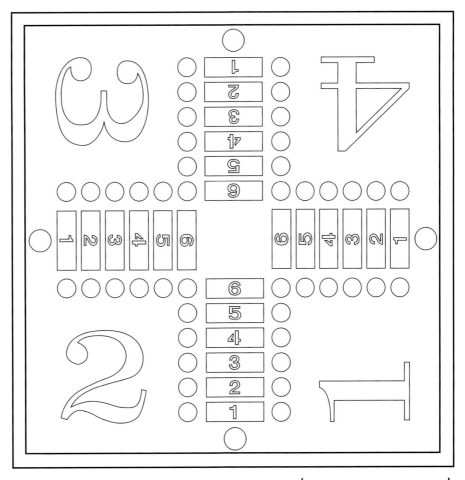

10"/25.4cm

Plain wooden chairs practically beg for a lick of paint. Try your hand at one (or all three) of these great options: a faux bamboo finish with stamped details, a rustic look accented with apple stencils that match the hutch on page 16, or folk-art inspired découpage.

BAMBOO CHAIR

You need: Wooden chair; all-purpose primer; acrylic craft paint in burnt sienna, cream, ochre and black; acrylic craft paint extender; small plastic cups; waterbase satin finish varnish; #120 and #220 sandpapers; tack cloth; 1"/2.5cm flat paint brush; #1 and #6 round artist's brushes; blue painter's tape.

Preparing surface: Sand using #120, then #220 sandpapers. Wipe clean with tack cloth. Using 1"/2.5cm brush, apply two coats of primer following label directions. Let dry thoroughly.

Sand with #220 sandpaper. Wipe clean with tack cloth.

Painting: Protect seat edge with painter's tape. Apply tape to uprights where they meet top and bottom back splats. Using 1"/2.5cm brush, apply two coats of burnt sienna to back splats, allowing each coat to dry before applying the next coat. Let dry two hours and remove tape. Continue to let dry overnight.

Apply tape to back splats where they meet uprights. In a cup, mix cream with $1/8$ part ochre. Using 1"/2.5cm brush, apply two coats of mixture, allowing each coat to dry before applying next coat. Let dry overnight. Do not remove tape.

Glazing: Make glaze by mixing burnt sienna in a cup with equal part water and ½ part extender. Using 1"/2.5cm brush, apply one thin coat to chair. Brush horizontally on horizontal pieces and vertically on vertical pieces. Add more water if mixture is not thin enough to make a haze of color, showing brush strokes over base coat. Let dry two hours and remove tape. Continue to let dry overnight.

Bamboo details: Use #1 brush

and black to make lines defining bamboo segments as shown. Let dry.

Make glaze by mixing one part burnt sienna in a cup with ½ part water and ½ part extender. Use #6 brush to make ovals as shown. Let dry thoroughly. Dip end of brush handle into black paint and touch to surface to make small black dots as shown. Let dry overnight.

Finishing: Using 1"/2.5cm brush, apply two coats of varnish, allowing each coat to dry before applying next coat. Let dry 24 hours before using.

YELLOW CHAIR WITH APPLE STENCIL

You need: Wooden chair; all-purpose primer; acrylic craft paints in yellow, red, dark green and brown; apple stencil to fit back

splats; stencil adhesive; waterbased semi-gloss finish varnish; #120 and #220 sandpapers; tack cloth; 1"/2.5cm flat paint brush; ¼"/.6cm and ½"/1.3cm stencil brushes; #1 and

#4 round artist's brushes; ruler; pencil; cellophane tape; scissors; paper plates; paper towels.

Preparing surface: Sand chair using #120, then #220 sandpapers. Wipe clean with tack cloth. Using

1"/2.5cm brush, apply one to two coats of primer following label directions. Let dry thoroughly. Sand with #220 sandpaper. Wipe clean with tack cloth.

Painting: Using 1"/2.5cm brush,

(Continued on page 70)

decorative chairs

(Continued from page 69)

apply two to three coats of yellow, allowing each coat to dry before applying next coat. For best results, lightly sand between coats using #220 sandpaper and wipe clean with tack cloth; do not sand after last coat. Let dry overnight.

Referring to photo, use #1 brush to paint two brown stems on front chair rail; let dry. Using #4 brush, paint two leaves dark green; let dry. Using end of brush handle, make two to three red dots between each leaf and stem; let dry.

Stenciling: Refer to stenciling how-tos on page 11. Measure and mark center of lower and upper back splats. On stencil, mask off all design elements around apples with tape. Spray wrong side of stencil with adhesive. Adhere stencil to lower splat so it is centered side to side and top leaf is approximately ½"/1.3cm from top edge. Using ½"/1.3cm stencil brush, stencil apples red. Carefully lift up stencil and position on upper splat, so it is centered side to side and top leaf is approximately ½"/1.3cm from top edge; stencil apples. Clean stencil before repositioning to prevent smudges. Let stenciling dry. Remove tape, then wash and dry stencil. Wash brush; let dry.

Mask off all design elements around leaves with tape. Spray wrong side of stencil with adhesive again if necessary. Adhere stencil to lower splat, lining up stencil over stenciled apples. Using ¼"/.6cm stencil brush, stencil leaves dark green. Stencil leaves on upper splat. Let stenciling dry. Remove tape, then wash and dry stencil.

Mask off all design elements around stems with tape. Adhere stencil to lower splat, lining up stencil over stenciled apples and leaves. Using ¼"/.6cm stencil brush, stencil stems brown. Stencil stems on upper splat. When all stenciling is completed, let dry overnight.

Finishing: Apply two coats of varnish, allowing each coat to dry before applying next coat. Let chair dry 24 hours before using.

BLUE CHAIR WITH DÉCOUPAGE

You need: Wooden chair; wallpaper border with motifs that fit chair's back splats; all-purpose primer; indoor/outdoor acrylic paint in turquoise and beige (or color to match background color of wallpaper border); acrylic craft paint in red or desired accent color; waterbased semi-gloss finish varnish; découpage medium; #120 and #220 sandpapers; tack cloth; 1"/2.5cm flat paint brush; ½"/1.3cm flat artist's brush; #1 round artist's brush; ruler; pencil; scissors; sheets of white paper large enough to fit back splats; cheesecloth.

Preparing surface: Sand chair using #120, then #220 sandpapers. Wipe clean with tack cloth. Using 1"/2.5cm brush, apply one to two coats of primer following label directions. Let dry thoroughly. Sand with #220 sandpaper. Wipe clean with tack cloth.

Painting: Using 1"/2.5cm brush for large areas and ½"/1.3cm brush for tight areas if chair has a woven seat, apply two to three coats of background color, allowing each coat to dry before applying next coat. For best results, lightly sand between coats using #220 sandpaper and wipe clean with tack cloth; do not sand after last coat. Working in the same manner, apply two to three coats of turquoise. Let dry overnight.

Weathering: Using #220 sandpaper, sand random areas down to background paint, as shown. Wipe clean with tack cloth.

Making patterns: Following contours of upper back splat, measure, mark and cut paper so it is about ⅜"/1cm to ½"/1.3cm smaller all around; as shown. Repeat for lower back splat.

Cutting wallpaper border: Place pattern for upper back splat on wallpaper border, centering it over one motif. Lightly trace around with pencil; cut out. Repeat for lower back splat.

Découpage: Using ½"/1.3cm brush, apply découpage medium to back of upper motif. Position on upper back splat and smooth with damp cheesecloth. Repeat for lower motif. Let dry four hours.

Accent painting: Using #1 brush and accent color, paint a narrow outline around each motif. Let dry overnight.

Finishing: Apply two coats of varnish, allowing each coat to dry before applying next coat. Let chair dry 24 hours before using.

Think out of the box with cute and colorful shelving and display spaces worthy of your treasures.

show offs

wonderful wall ideas

Wood and wallpaper scraps make it easy to whip up a one-of-a-kind project. Once sponge-painted, this clever key cabinet is papered inside and out with a striped design and completed with a self-stick fruit motif.

You need: Wooden key cabinet with recessed panel door and wooden knob; piece of pre-pasted striped wallpaper; self-stick border with fruit motif; all-purpose primer; acrylic paint in light, medium and dark colors to match wallpaper; waterbased satin finish varnish; screwdriver; #120 and #220 sandpapers; tack cloth; ½"/1.3cm flat artist's brush; small sea sponge; paper plates; paper towels; pencil; ruler; small, sharp scissors; three cup hooks.

Preparing surface: Remove knob. Sand all surfaces to be painted using #120, then #220 sandpapers. Wipe clean with tack cloth. Apply one coat of primer following label directions. Let dry thoroughly. Sand with #220 sand-paper. Wipe clean with tack cloth.

Painting: Allowing each coat to dry thoroughly before applying the next coat, apply two to three coats of darkest color to cabinet and lightest color to knob. For best results, lightly sand between coats using #220 sandpaper and wipe clean with tack cloth; do not sand after last coat. When all painting is completed, let dry overnight.

Sponge-painting: Wet sponge, then wring out until almost dry. Pour lightest color onto paper plate. Pounce sponge into paint, then pounce onto paper towel to remove excess paint. Pouncing to apply paint, sponge-paint outside surfaces only, omitting recessed door panel; let dry. Wash sponge well. Working in the same manner, sponge-paint cabinet and knob using medium color. Let dry overnight.

Finishing: Apply two coats of varnish (except for recessed door panel and inside back panel of cabinet), allowing each coat to dry before applying next coat. Let dry 24 hours.

Wallpaper accents: Measure, mark and cut striped wallpaper to fit inside recessed door panel and inside back panel of cabinet. Adhere wallpaper pieces in place; let dry. Cut out fruit motif. Adhere in place.

Assembling: Install knob. Install cup hooks to inside back panel of cabinet for keys.

SPONGING

Sponging is one of the quickest and easiest techniques to create an uneven wash of paint. Before you begin, always rinse sea sponges in water and squeeze out the excess so sponge is as dry as possible. Dip the sponge into thinned paint and remove excess on paper towel. Allow some areas of the sponge to retain more paint than others. Dab sponge around the surface, changing direction often, and overlapping and building up an uneven coat of paint. Dab your sponge in some areas but use the sponge to "brush" on the paint in other areas. Soften the sponge brush lines by dabbing with a drier area of the sponge.

harvest key cabinet

Showcase your favorite china in perky plate shelves coated in shades that pick up their patterns. Paint each a different color, then "weather" slightly for a homey, rustic feel that's perfect for pottery.

You need: Two wooden plate rail shelves; all-purpose primer; indoor/outdoor acrylic paint in beige, orange and green; waterbased satin finish varnish (optional, see finishing); #120 and #220 sandpapers; tack cloth; 1"/2.5cm flat paint brush; three large cup hooks.

Preparing surface: Sand shelves using #120, then #220 sandpapers. Wipe clean with tack cloth. Apply one coat of primer following label directions. Let dry thoroughly. Sand with #220 sandpaper. Wipe clean with tack cloth.

Painting: Apply two coats of beige to shelves. For best results, lightly sand between coats using #220 sandpaper and wipe clean with tack cloth; do not sand after second coat. Working in the same manner, apply two coats of orange to one shelf and green to other shelf. Let dry overnight.

Weathering: Using #220 sandpaper, sand random areas down to beige paint. Wipe clean with tack cloth.

Finishing: For a rustic look, do not varnish. For a finished look, apply two coats of varnish to shelves, allowing each coat to dry before applying next coat. Let dry 24 hours before using. Install three cup hooks into bottom of green shelf, as shown.

SURFACE PREPPING

If the chosen surface has been previously finished with a clear shellac or varnish, you may choose to use steel wool rather than sand paper to prepare the surface. Steel wool also works well on very irregular or rounded surfaces such as chair legs and bedposts, and on bare soft wood surfaces such as balsa or white pine. Follow the same procedure as for using sandpaper, and remember to check for fibers that may be left behind before proceeding to the next step. Be sure to wear protective gloves to protect your skin from steel fibers.

sunny plate shelves

You need: Wooden shelf; all-purpose primer; indoor/outdoor acrylic paint in color shown or as desired; waterbased satin finish varnish; #120 and #220 sandpapers; tack cloth; 1"/2.5cm flat paint brush; mounting hardware and power drill with bit (see mounting to wall).

Preparing surface: Sand using #120, then #220 sandpapers. Wipe clean with tack cloth. Apply one coat of primer following label directions. Let dry thoroughly. Sand with #220 sandpaper. Wipe clean with tack cloth.

Painting: Apply two to three coats of paint, allowing each coat to dry before applying next coat. For best results, lightly sand between coats using #220 sandpaper and wipe clean with tack cloth; do not sand after last coat. Let dry overnight.

Finishing: Apply two coats of varnish, allowing each coat to dry before applying next coat. Let dry 24 hours before using.

Mounting to wall: Do not mount shelf near an outlet or wall switch to avoid electric wiring. For plaster walls, use plastic wall anchors matched to size of provided shelf screws, drilling holes using bit to match size of anchors. For sheet rock walls, use toggle bolts, drilling holes using bit to match size of bolts.

Paint and plants bring the beauty of a sunny window ledge indoors. Coat an unfinished wooden shelf in a hue suggestive of the season, then pair with pots in a similiar color scheme for a tone-on-tone effect.

lovely ledges

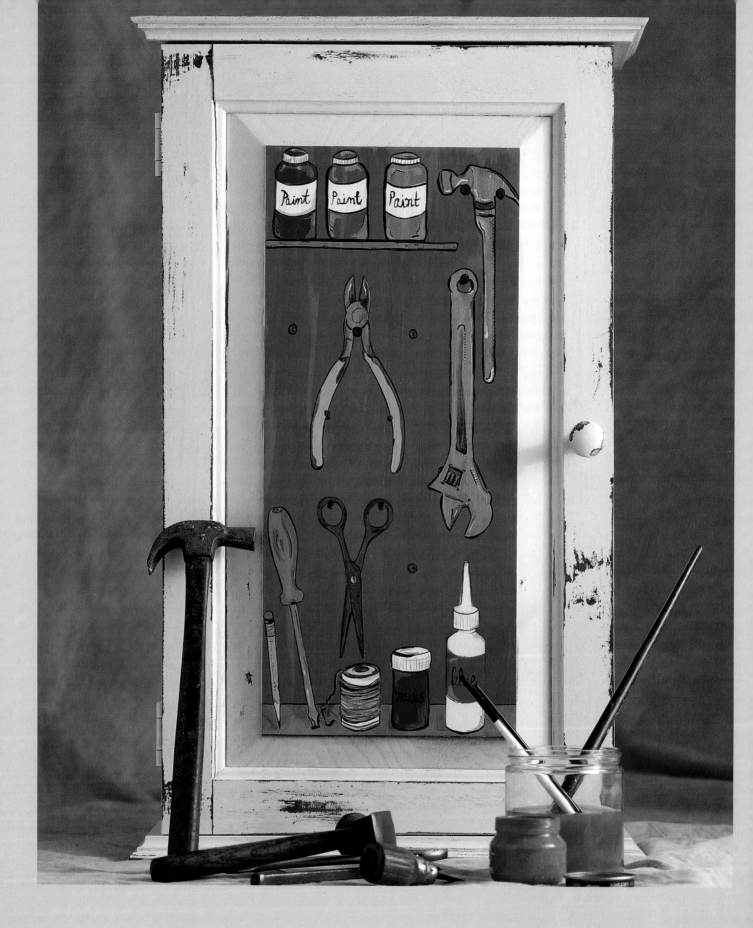

There's no mystery to what's hidden behind this cabinet door. Use a pencil to trace the outline of tools and other fix-it supplies, then fill in with acrylic paints. Copy the idea for sewing notions, baking supplies or any other hobby.

You need: Wooden cabinet with raised panel door and wooden knob; all-purpose primer; acrylic craft paint in medium blue, black, white, bright yellow, dark yellow, dark orange, dark pink, purple, light gray, medium gray, light brown, and medium brown; waterbased satin finish varnish; screwdriver; #120 and #220 sandpapers; tack cloth; artist's brushes: ¼"/.6cm and ½"/ 1.3cm flat, and #1 and #3 round; ruler; pencil; black graphite paper.

Preparing surface: Remove knob, door and hardware; set hardware aside. Sand all surfaces to be painted using #120, then #220 sandpapers. Wipe clean with tack cloth. Using ½"/1.3cm brush, apply one coat of primer following label directions. Let dry thoroughly. Sand with #220 sandpaper. Wipe clean

with tack cloth.

Painting: Using ½"/1.3cm brush, apply two to three coats of blue to raised door panel, allowing each coat to dry thoroughly before applying the next coat. For best results, lightly sand between coats using #220 sandpaper and wipe clean with tack cloth; do not sand after last coat. Working in the same manner, apply two coats of black to knob and remaining surfaces, then two coats of white. When all painting is completed, let dry overnight.

Weathering: Using #220 sandpaper, sand areas which would naturally receive the most wear, like edges, handles, etc. Sand down to black paint as shown. Wipe clean with tack cloth.

Painting door panel: Enlarge pattern on a photo copier to fit

size of your door panel. Transfer pattern to panel using graphite paper. Refer to photo for suggested color placement. Paint white areas first, color areas second, shading and highlighting third, and black outlines and writing fourth. Use ¼"/.6cm and #3 brushes for large areas and #1 brush for small details. Work one section at a time and let section dry before proceeding to next section. When all painting is completed, let dry overnight.

Finishing: Using ½"/1.3cm brush, apply two coats of varnish to all surfaces, allowing each coat to dry before applying next coat. Let dry 24 hours before using.

Assembling: Install hardware, rehang door, then install knob.

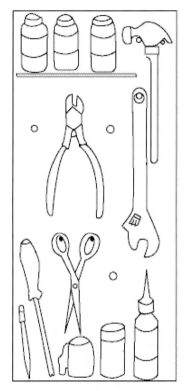

tool cabinet

You need: Wooden shelf with doors, wooden knobs and chicken wire inserts; all-purpose primer; acrylic craft paint in cream, burgundy, dark ochre and olive green; waterbased satin finish varnish; mini checkerboard stencil; stencil adhesive; découpage glue; découpage paper with right-facing and left-facing chicken motifs, or desired motifs that fit inside checkerboard pattern; small, sharp scissors; screwdriver; #120 and #220 sandpapers; tack cloth; artist's brushes: #1 round and ⅛"/.3cm, ¼"/.6cm and ½"/1.3cm flat; ½"/1.3cm stencil brush; craft knife; straight edge ruler; cutting mat; 1½"/3.8cm-wide blue painter's tape; paper plate; paper towels; cheesecloth.

Preparing surface: Remove knobs, doors, hardware and chicken wire; set hardware and chicken wire aside. Sand all surfaces to be painted using #120, then #220 sandpapers. Wipe clean with tack cloth. Using ½"/1.3cm brush, apply one coat of primer following label directions. Let dry thoroughly. Sand with #220 sandpaper. Wipe clean with tack cloth.

Painting: Using ½"/1.3cm brush, apply two to three coats of paint, allowing each coat to dry thoroughly before applying the next coat. For best results, lightly sand between coats using #220 sandpaper and wipe clean with tack cloth; do not sand after last coat. Paint one section a time, allowing section to dry before proceeding to next section. Paint front, doors and inside recessed windows at sides cream. Paint top and bottom burgundy. Paint sides and inside cubby hole dark ochre. Paint knobs olive green. Let dry overnight.

Painting checkerboard front: Determine size of squares by measuring width and height of front. If you have to fudge along height, make adjustments at side edges of doors, as shown. Working on cutting mat, cut painter's tape into squares using craft knife and straight edge. Adhere squares to front in a checkerboard pattern. Using ¼"/.6cm brush, paint squares burgundy, dark ochre and olive, alternating colors as shown. Let dry four hours. Remove tape, then continue to dry overnight.

Stenciling checkerboard doors: Refer to stenciling how-tos on page 11. Spray wrong side of mini checkerboard stencil with adhesive. Adhere stencil to door front. Using stencil brush, stencil checkerboard burgundy. Carefully lift up stencil, wipe clean of wet paint, and position on second door. Stencil second door in the same manner. Let dry. Using ⅛"/.3cm flat brush, continue checkerboard pattern around front inside edges of doors by painting similar size squares. Let dry overnight.

Découpage: Cut out right-facing and left-facing chicken motifs. Use ½"/1.3cm brush to apply découpage glue to back of each motif. Referring to photo, adhere motifs to checkerboard squares, smoothing with damp cheese cloth. Working in the same manner; adhere motifs to inside door openings and recessed windows at sides. Let dry two hours.

Accent painting: Using #1 brush and dark ochre, paint chicken scratch tracks for motifs inside door openings and recessed windows at sides; as shown. Let dry overnight.

Finishing: Apply two coats of varnish to all surfaces, allowing each coat to dry before applying next coat. Let dry 24 hours before using.

Assembling: Replace chicken wire and hardware. Rehang doors, then install knobs.

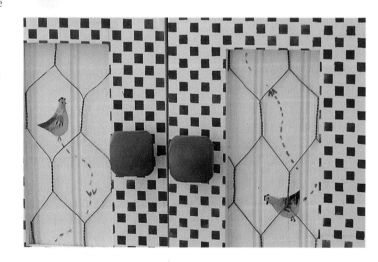

Painted with a checkerboard of happy hens, this country cupboard offers plenty of neat nooks for storage and display. Shelves sit behind the chicken-wire doors and the cubby below offers space for cookbooks, spices or tea tins.

checkerboard cupboard

Recycle a window-paned door into a smart garden center. Paint a bright shade of blue then add shelves, pegs and hooks to store tools, pots, seeds and other yard-beautifying supplies. Maximize space by hanging an apron from a shovel and stuff gloves and other small items in the apron pockets.

You need: Old wooden door; four wooden shelf brackets; two 8"/20.3cm-deep wooden shelves cut 3"/7.6cm wider than door; seven unfinished wooden screw-in Shaker pegs; two metal coat hooks; all-purpose primer; indoor/outdoor acrylic semi-gloss paint in dark turquoise and brown; glazing medium for acrylic paint; exterior grade waterbased polyurethane varnish; #100, #120 and #220 sandpapers; tack cloth; 3"/7.6cm flat paint brush; 6"/15.2cm wallpaper paste brush; blue painter's tape; small paint bucket; paper towels.

Preparing surface: Sand door using first #100, then #120 and #220 sandpapers. Sand shelf brackets, shelves and Shaker pegs using #120, then #220 sandpapers. Wipe all clean with tack cloth. Install brackets and Shaker pegs on door as shown. Apply painter's tape to glass on both sides of door, butting tape to frame. Apply one to two coats of primer to all surfaces following label directions. Let dry thoroughly. Sand with #220 sandpaper. Wipe clean with tack cloth.

Painting: Apply two to three coats of dark turquoise, allowing each coat to dry before applying the next coat. For best results, lightly sand between coats using #220 sandpaper and wipe clean with tack cloth; do not sand after last coat. Let dry overnight.

Dragging: To make glaze, mix one part brown paint with four parts glazing medium in bucket. Working a section at a time, brush on mixture then drag dry wallpaper brush across the surface with the grain of the wood. Drag horizontally on horizontal parts and vertically on vertical parts. Wipe brush on paper towels to remove excess glaze. Keep brushing in same direction until the desired effect is achieved, then move on to another section. Let dry overnight.

Finishing: Apply two coats of varnish to all pieces, allowing each coat to dry before applying next coat. Let dry 2 hours and remove tape. Continue to let dry 24 hours before using.

Assembling: Install metal coat hooks at top of door. Position shelves on shelf brackets.

garden door

Bold brushstrokes, faux finishes and smart stenciling turn everyday items into designer-style showpieces.

easy accessories

planters, clocks, trays and more

You need: Wooden canister set (A: tall and wide, B: tall and narrow, C: medium, and D: short); unfinished wooden fruit: pear, large apple, small apple and peach; all-purpose primer; acrylic craft paint in green, white, red, blue, yellow and dark brown; acrylic craft paint extender; paper plates; waterbased matte finish varnish; #120 and #220 sandpapers; tack cloth; 1"/2.5cm flat paintbrush; #1 round artist's brush; power drill with $^{11}/_{64}$"/.4cm drill bit; five #8 x 1¼"/3.2cm wood screws; screwdriver; tape measure; pencil; blue painter's tape; craft knife; straight edge ruler; cutting mat; cheese cloth.

Drilling holes: Drill hole through center of each canister lid and into center bottom of fruit.

Preparing surface: Sand canisters and fruit using #120, then #220 sandpapers. Wipe clean with tack cloth. Using flat brush, apply one to two coats of primer to all surfaces following label directions. Let dry thoroughly. Sand with #220 sandpaper. Wipe clean with tack cloth.

Measure around lid A, and mark for evenly spaced narrow green and wide yellow vertical stripes. Use strips of painter's tape to cover yellow stripe areas. Cut strips to size on cutting mat using straight edge and craft knife. Repeat for lid C, marking for wide red and narrower light green stripes. Cover light green stripe areas with tape. Measure height of lid B, subtract ¼"/.6cm and divide by two. This is the size of the light green square areas. Cut squares of tape and space around lid as shown. Repeat for yellow square areas on lid D.

Painting canisters: Using flat brush, apply two coats of paint to each piece, allowing each coat to dry before applying the next coat.

Canister A: Paint lid and bottom green. Canister B: On paper plate, mix green with $^1/_4$ part white and paint top of lid and bottom. Paint lid rim red. Canister C: Paint lid and bottom red.

Canister D: On paper plate, mix blue with ½ part white and paint lid and bottom. Let dry four hours and remove tape.

Tape over painted areas adjacent to unpainted areas. Paint lid A stripes yellow. Paint lid B squares and lid C stripes using light green paint mixture. Paint lid D squares yellow. Let dry two hours and remove tape. Continue to let dry overnight.

Color-washing canisters: Tape over adjacent areas as needed. Mix glazes on paper plate and dip cheese cloth into glaze. Wipe cloth on surface to apply color. Use damp cloth to wipe off excess color as needed. To layer colors, allow first color to dry before applying the next. Make white, yellow, green and blue glazes by mixing one part paint with one part water and one part extender. Canister A: Color-wash green areas with white and yellow.

Color-wash yellow areas with white. Canister B: Color-wash light green areas with green, white and yellow. Canister C: Color-wash red and light green areas with yellow. Canister D: Color-wash light blue areas with white and blue. Color-wash yellow areas with white. Let dry overnight.

Painting fruit: Paint pear yellow, large apple red and small apple green. Mix one part yellow with ¼ part white and paint peach. Mix color-wash glazes same as for canisters. Color-wash pear with green, large apple with white, small apple with red and peach with white. Use round brush to paint pear and apple stems dark brown. Let dry overnight.

Assembling: Screw fruit onto canister lids.

Finishing: Using flat brush, apply two coats of varnish, allowing each coat to dry before applying next coat. Let dry 24 hours before using.

Cylindrical wood boxes are ideal for storing sugar, flour and other kitchen counter essentials. Add some interest by color-washing old canisters, then stencil a geometric pattern on the lid rims. Complete by attaching fun, fruit-shaped wood knobs to the lids.

cool canisters

You need: Wooden boat oar; four white canvas totes; four metal coat hooks and screws; all-purpose primer; indoor/outdoor high-gloss acrylic paint in white and navy blue; acrylic craft paint in navy blue; textile medium for acrylic paint; nautical stencil and alphabet stencil to fit tote as shown; stencil adhesive; four pieces of cardboard that fit snugly inside totes; #120 and #220 sandpapers; tack cloth; 1"/2.5cm flat paintbrush; 1"/2.5cm stencil brush; 1"/2.5cm-wide blue painter's tape; masking tape; ruler; power drill; ⅛"/3mm drillbit; screwdriver; paper plate; paper towels; iron.

Installing hooks: Measure and mark for spacing of hooks. Use a drill to make pilot holes for screws. Install hooks using screws.

Preparing wood surface: Sand using #120, then #220 sandpapers. Wipe clean with tack cloth. Apply one to two coats of primer, including hooks, following label directions. Let dry thoroughly. Sand with #220 sandpaper. Wipe clean with tack cloth.

Painting oar: Apply two to three coats of white to oar and hooks, allowing each coat to dry before applying next coat. Let dry overnight.

Paint hand grip navy blue. To form stripes at paddle end, apply three strips of painter's tape beginning 1½"/3.8cm from end and spacing them 1"/2.5cm apart. Paint end and two stripes navy blue. Let last coat dry two hours, then remove tape. Continue to let dry overnight.

Stenciling totes: Refer to stenciling how-tos on page 11. Insert cardboard into each tote. Using masking tape, tape each tote to work surface making sure fabric lies flat and taut. Spray wrong side of nautical stencil with adhesive, then adhere to first tote. Mix textile medium with navy blue craft paint following label directions. Using stencil brush, stencil motif. Carefully lift up stencil and position on second tote. Clean stencil before repositioning to prevent smudges. Stencil second tote in the same manner. Continue until all totes are stenciled. Wash and dry stencil brush. Let totes dry six hours, then stencil letters. Let dry overnight.

Heat setting: Use iron to heat-set totes following textile medium directions.

Keep the bath or poolside shipshape by organizing toys, towels and other necessities in roomy canvas totes stenciled with letters and seaworthy motifs. An old oar painted white with blue and navy stripes serves as a holding point; simply screw in hooks to accommodate the bags.

stenciled totes

Small pots of fragrant herbs look lovely arranged in a rustic wooden tray. Purchase an unfinished style at your local craft store or recycle a flea-market find. Coat it with a light wash of bright paint, then sand lightly for a distressed look.

PLANT TRAY

You need: Wooden tray; acrylic paint in red; waterbased satin finish varnish (optional, see finishing); #120 and #220 sandpapers; tack cloth; ½"/1.3cm flat artist's brush.

Preparing surface: Sand tray using #120, then #220 sand-papers. Wipe clean with tack cloth.

Painting: Apply two to three coats of red, allowing each coat to dry before applying next coat. Let dry overnight.

Weathering: Using #220 sandpaper, sand random areas down to raw wood. Wipe clean with tack cloth.

Finishing: For a rustic look, do not varnish. For a finished look, apply two coats of varnish to tray, allowing each coat to dry before applying next coat. Let dry 24 hours before using.

SPONGED FLOWER POTS

You need: Two clay pots to fit inside planter; all-purpose primer; acrylic craft paint in off white, yellow, red and dark blue; waterbased satin finish varnish; ½"/1.3cm flat artist's brush; small sea sponge; paper plates; paper towels.

Priming: Apply one coat of primer to outside and inside of each pot following label directions. Let dry thoroughly.

Painting: Apply two to three coats of paint allowing each coat to dry thoroughly before applying next coat. Paint inside and outside of each pot, painting inside the same color used for rim.

For pot with red sponge-painted rim (pot A), paint rim yellow and bottom off white. For pot with yellow sponge-painted rim (pot B), paint rim off white and bottom yellow. After all painting is completed, let dry overnight.

Sponge-painting: Wet sponge, then wring out until almost dry. Brush color onto paper plate. Pounce sponge into paint, then pounce onto paper towel to remove excess paint. Pounce to apply paint. Change direction of sponge to vary texture. Let each color dry before apply the next color. Wash sponge well between colors.

For pot A, sponge-paint bottom yellow, then rim red. For pot B, sponge-paint bottom dark blue, then rim yellow. Let dry overnight.

Finishing: Apply two coats of varnish, allowing each coat to dry before applying next coat. Let dry 24 hours before using.

plant tray and flowerpots

VINE WATERING CAN

You need: Galvanized watering can; all-purpose primer; acrylic paint in white, dark brown and dark green; 1"/2.5cm flat paintbrush; #3 and #6 round artist's brushes; pencil; aerosol satin lacquer.

Preparing watering can: If watering can is not new, wash well to remove dirt and debris. Let dry completely. Remove sprinkle nozzle; set aside.

Priming: Using 1"/2.5cm brush, apply one to two coats of primer to outside of watering can, allowing first coat to dry before applying the next. Let dry overnight.

Painting: Using 1"/2.5cm brush, apply two coats of white acrylic paint, allowing first coat to dry before applying second coat. Let dry overnight.

Referring to photo for suggested design, lightly pencil vine line, making sure to allow room for leaves. Using #3 brush, paint vine line dark brown; let dry. Using #6 brush, paint leaves dark green; let dry.

Mix white with dark green to make a lighter green. Paint leaf veins using #3 brush. Let dry overnight.

Finishing: Referring to label directions, apply two coats of lacquer to outside of watering can, allowing first coat to dry before applying the second coat. Let dry 24 hours before using.

Assembling: Attach nozzle.

MELON WATERING CAN

You need: Galvanized watering can; all-purpose primer; acrylic paint in dark pink, dark green, black and white; 1"/2.5cm flat paintbrush; ½"/1.3cm flat and #6 round artist's brushes; ruler; pencil; aerosol satin lacquer.

Preparing watering can: If watering can is not new, wash well to remove dirt and debris. Let dry completely. Remove sprinkle nozzle; set aside.

Priming: Using 1"/2.5cm brush, apply one to two coats of primer to outside of watering can, allowing first coat to dry before applying the next. Let dry overnight.

Painting: Refer to photo for color placement. Measure, then lightly mark guidelines for painting stripes. Use 1"/2.5cm brush for larger areas and ½"/1.3cm brush for stripes. Apply two to three coats of paint to each section, allowing first coat to dry before applying second coat. Paint white first, pink second and green third. Using #6 brush, paint seeds black.

Let dry overnight.

Finishing: Referring to label directions, apply two coats of lacquer to outside of watering can, allowing first coat to dry before applying the second coat. Let dry 24 hours before using.

Assembling: Attach nozzle.

A little paint transforms a galvanized watering can into a picture-perfect container for fresh flowers or a potted plant. Do a graceful vine or a stylized watermelon, then set one or two on the front steps or on the side porch for passers-by to admire.

watering cans

You need: 9¾"/24.1cm round of ⅜"/10mm-thick exterior grade plywood with one good face; 12"/30.5cm-diameter grape vine wreath with 7½"/19cm opening; twelve clay pots, 1½"/3.8cm-diameter by 1½"/3.8cm-high; all-purpose primer; acrylic craft paint in green, golden yellow, orange, magenta, pink, purple, cobalt blue and white; acrylic craft paint extender; exterior grade waterbased polyurethane varnish; ½"/1.3cm flat paintbrush; #1 round artist's brush; pencil; straight edge ruler; power drill with ⅚₁₆"/.15cm and ⅛"/.3cm drill bits; #20 gauge stainless steel wire; wire cutters; clock movement with shaft for ⅜"/ 1cm-thick dial; clock movement cover to protect movement from weather; clock hand set with 3"/7.6cm long minute hand; 1¾"/4.4cm long second hand; paper plate; cheese cloth; weather proof silicone glue; small wood flower picks; Spanish moss.

Drilling holes: Locate center of plywood round. Drill hole through plywood using ⅚₁₆"/.15cm drill bit. Draw line from an edge, through center, to opposite edge. Draw another line, perpendicular to first, from edge through center, to opposite edge, dividing face into four equal parts. At each line, ½"/1.3cm from edge, mark for two holes, each ¼"/.6cm from either side of line. Drill holes through plywood using ⅛"/.3cm drill bit.

Priming clock face: Using flat brush, apply one to two coats of primer to both sides following label directions. Let dry thoroughly. Sand with #220 sandpaper. Wipe clean with tack cloth.

Painting clock face: Apply two to three coats of green paint to both sides, allowing each coat to dry thoroughly before applying the next coat. Let dry overnight.

Glazing clock face: To make glaze, mix one part golden yellow with one part water and one part extender on paper plate. Dip cheese cloth into glaze and pounce cloth lightly on good face of plywood to apply color. Let dry overnight.

Finishing clock face: Using flat brush, apply two coats of varnish to both sides, allowing each coat to dry before applying next coat. Let dry overnight.

Painting flower pots: Using flat brush, apply two to three coats of paint allowing each coat to dry thoroughly before applying next coat. Paint two pots each golden yellow, orange, magenta, pink, purple and cobalt blue. Using round brush, paint white numbers, matching pot color and angles of numbers to photograph. Let dry overnight.

Finishing flower pots: Using flat brush, apply two coats of varnish, allowing each coat to dry before applying next coat. Let dry overnight.

Assembling: For each pot, thread a 10"/25.4cm length of wire through drainage hole and out top of pot. Adjust wire so ends are even. Bend ends at right angles to top and bottom of pot. Thread wire ends through wreath and twist together at back of wreath to secure. Cut off excess wire and tuck twisted end into wreath. Refer to photo for placement of pots.

At each pair of holes at edge of clock face, thread both ends of 10"/25.4cm length of wire from back of face to front. Adjust wire so ends are even. Place clock face behind wreath. Thread wire ends through wreath so they exit at front of wreath and close to a flower pot. Twist ends together to secure, cut off excess wire and tuck twisted end into wreath.

Following package directions, secure clock movement to clock face along with hands and movement cover.

Decorating: Use silicone glue to adhere bunches of wooden flower picks and tufts of Spanish moss into each pot. If used outside, hang in a protected area. Let dry 24 hours before using.

A grapevine wreath fitted with mini-flower pots offers a delightful way to mark the hours. Paint the pots in a variety of warm-weather hues, fill with wooden blooms and Spanish moss, then wire to the wreath. Attach to a clockwork background painted bright green and take time out to enjoy your work.

garden clock

Transforming a dull mailbox into a one-of-a-kind work of art is easier than you might think. The secret lies in using self-adhesive tapes that are precut in zig-zag, scallop and other shapes. These will give you the wonderful wavy stripes.

You need: Plastic mailbox; all-purpose primer; Aleene's Premium-Coat Acrylics in True Blue; waterbased satin finish varnish; ½"/1.3cm flat artist's brush; #220 sandpaper; tack cloth; measuring tape; scissors; Plaid Fun Paint Shape Tape in various widths and colors.

Preparing surface: Apply one coat of primer to outside of mailbox. Let dry.

Painting: Apply two coats of blue, allowing each coat to dry before applying next coat. For best results, lightly sand between coats and wipe clean with tack cloth; do not sand after last coat. Let dry overnight.

Measure around mailbox, from bottom edge of one side to bottom edge of other side. Cut tapes to length. Refer to photo for stripe widths and color placement. Working one stripe at a time, adhere tapes, then paint stripe. Let dry; remove tapes. Continue in this manner until all stripes are painted. Let dry overnight.

Finishing: Apply two coats of varnish, allowing each coat to dry before applying next coat. Let dry 24 hours before using.

TIP

To leave a brush for a short time without cleaning it (say, when taking a lunch break!), wrap the brush in foil or a plastic bag to keep it soft and pliable. To leave it for longer periods of time without cleaning, wrap it in plastic and put it in the freezer.

striped mailbox

They say neatness begins at home. Prepare your little one for the classroom or coatroom with a painted pine hook board ideal for hanging coats and book bags. Pastel paints and a wire "smokestack" lend charm to the design.

You need: 20"/51cm-length of 1" x 10"/2.5cm x 25.5cm clear pine; acrylic craft paint in desired colors; #220 sandpaper; tack cloth; artist's brushes: #3 and #6 round and ½"/1.3mm flat; saber saw; aluminum flashing; tin snips; staple gun; power drill with ⅛"/3mm bit; 24"/61cm-length of ³⁄₁₆"/5mm armature wire; four metal coat hooks; screwdriver; large nail; two 2"/5cm sawtooth hangers with nails; hammer.

Cutting wood: Enlarge pattern (at right) to 20"/51cm across. Trace on pine; cut out. Sand.

Painting: Paint rack as desired; let dry.

Finishing: Cut flashing to fit front and sides of roof peaks; cut flashing slightly wider than wood. Wrap flashing around peaks; staple at back. Use nail to press designs in flashing. Paint if desired. Drill three holes in top of chimney. Cut wire into three pieces; curl one end of each; insert in holes for smoke. Attach coat hooks to front of rack.

Hanging: Use hammer to secure a sawtooth hanger below the roof peaks, on either side of back.

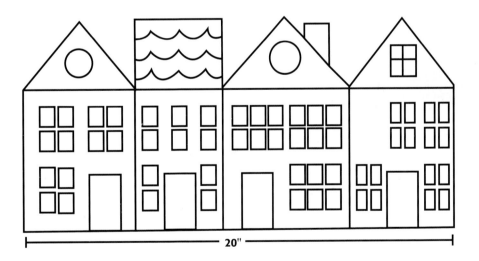

20"

rowhouse coatrack

You need: 9" x 14"/22.9cm x 35.6cm wooden tray with wooden handles; four 5"/12.7cm-diameter x ⅜"/10mm-thick unfinished wooden coasters; all-purpose primer; acrylic craft paint in white, green, red and black; waterbased satin finish varnish; #120 and #220 sandpapers; tack cloth; screwdriver; 1"/2.5cm flat paintbrush; #0, #1 and #6 round artist's brushes; tracing paper, pencil, black graphite paper; masking tape.

Preparing surface: Remove handles. Sand all surfaces of tray, handles and coasters, using #120, then #220 sandpapers. Wipe clean with tack cloth. Using flat brush, apply one to two coats of primer to all surfaces following label directions. Let dry thoroughly.

Sand with #220 sandpaper. Wipe clean with tack cloth.

Painting tray: Using flat brush, apply two to three coats of white to tray and green to handles, allowing each coat to dry before applying the next coat. For best results, lightly sand between coats using #220 sandpaper and wipe clean with tack cloth; do not sand after last coat. Let dry overnight.

Trace two corner leaf patterns, four triple leaf patterns and five lady bug patterns. Space patterns on long side of tray as shown. Tape into position. Slip graphite paper under each pattern and go over lines to transfer. Transfer only outline of lady bugs at this point. Repeat for other long side. Tape two corner leaf patterns on short side of tray as shown

and transfer. Repeat for other side.

Using #6 brush, paint leaves green and lady bugs red, applying two coats. Let dry thoroughly. Transfer lady bug details to lady bugs. Using #0 brush, paint details black. Let dry overnight.

Painting coasters: Using flat brush, apply two to three coats of red to both sides of coasters. For best results, lightly sand between coats using #220 sandpaper and wipe clean with tack cloth; do not

sand after last coat. Let dry overnight.

Trace coaster pattern and transfer lines to coasters. Paint pattern black, using #1 brush for small lines and #6 brush for large areas. Let dry overnight.

Finishing: Using flat brush, apply two coats of varnish to tray, handles and coasters, allowing each coat to dry before applying next coat. Let dry 24 hours before using.

Assembling: Install handles.

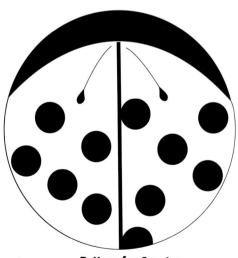

Pattern for Coaster
enlarge 200%

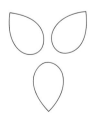

Pattern for Triple Leaf
enlarge 200%

Pattern for Corner Leaf
enlarge 200%

Pattern for Lady Bug
actual size

Drink up! Serve up iced tea or flavored lemonade on a summer-friendly tray with matching coasters They're easy to create with simple templates and make a great addition to any outdoor gathering.

ladybug tray and coaster set

You need: White ceramic cups, bowls, plates or other pieces; enamel paints in light, medium and dark shades of desired color, white and bright yellow; paintbrushes: 1"/2.5cm flat, ¼"/6cm round, fine artist's; clear adhesive contact paper; tracing paper; pencil; scissors; ruler; clean, lint-free cloths; paper plates; pin or fine-tipped awl; graphite pouncer (for transferring design).

1 Sketch a simple flower pattern. Place a square of tracing paper on top and puncture sketch lines with pin or fine-tipped awl. Increase or decrease size of flower design as needed to fit on various pieces.

2 Measure and mark a square of self-adhesive paper for each ceramic piece to be painted, making sure squares are approximately the same size as each flower pattern. Cut out squares.

3 Peel paper backing off each square. Place squares where desired on each ceramic piece. Rub corners of each square to ensure that edges adhere, preventing paint from seeping under square outlines.

4 On a paper plate or palette, mix your base color paint with an equal amount of water to create a semi-transparent glaze. Stir together with a paintbrush.

5 Wipe brush clean, then add a dollop of white paint to your base glaze and blend slightly. The less you mix, the more of a washed, streaked effect will be achieved.

6 Using a flat, wide brush, paint entire piece including masked-off square to maintain the square's sharp, crisp edges. Keep strokes consistent for a uniform appearance.

7 Lightly blow on ceramic surface until dry. Carefully peel off self-adhesive paper square. Gently clean off any sticky residue left behind.

8 Place perforated flower drawing in center of square. Using pouncing tool, transfer flower to ceramic piece. Blow lightly on piece to remove any excess dust from tracing paper.

9 Remove flower template from center of piece, pulling up from one side. Try not to disrupt any pounced pigment. Transfer pattern to each piece in same way.

10 Using yellow paint and round brush, paint flower. Carefully paint outline, then use smooth, even strokes to fill in centers of individual petals. Let dry.

11 Using medium shade of paint and flat brush, paint band around edge of piece. Keep a steady hand, and paint with long, smooth strokes.

12 Using a clean, lint-free cloth, smooth paint into an even band, removing all excess pigment. Let dry.

13 Using darkest shade of paint and round brush, paint narrow, evenly-spaced stripes along outer bands; let dry.

14 Use dark paint to fill centers of flower motifs with a small circle. Following manufacturer's directions, heat-set paint.

Enamel paints take so-so ceramics from white to bright. It all starts with porcelain plates, cups and saucers, and china-friendly paints. Brush on soft pastel background, then detail with sunny flower blossoms and sweet stripes.

cheerful ceramics

Go wild painting bold zebra stripes, leopard spots, cheetah prints and tortoise shells on wood and papier mâché boxes, vases, flowerpots, you name it! The techniques are easy to master; group your finished pieces on a table top to create your own wilderness preserve.

Practice making an assortment of eye-catching animal finishes. Look around your home for photographs, prints and objects to use for inspiration. Follow the same steps to make stencils, or try your hand painting zebra and tiger stripes freehand.

You need (for each box):

Wooden box; Paint palette or plate

GIRAFFE-PRINT

Note: See below, steps 1-3

You need: Acrylic paints in yellow, brown and black; stencil blank; fine-point black permanent marker; craft knife; masking tape; stencil brush; picture of giraffe for reference; polyurethane varnish.

TORTOISESHELL FINISH

Note: See below, steps 4-6

You need: Glazing medium for oil paints; oil paints in raw sienna, burnt sienna and burnt umber; acrylic paint in yellow; paintbrushes: #2 round and 1"/2.5cm badger; polyurethane varnish.

GIRAFFE-PRINT

1 **Paint a box and lid yellow; let dry. Draw giraffe spots on the stencil blank with a permanent marker. Carefully cut out spots using a very sharp craft knife. Leave a wide border around the outer edge of stencil.**

2 **Tape stencil to the side of box. On the palette, mix a small amount of brown and black paint to make very deep, dark brown. Dip stencil brush in paint; blot excess. Dab brush straight up and down inside cutout areas of stencil. Remove stencil, clean thoroughly.**

3 **Move the stencil to the next position; space spots evenly and following in the same direction. Continue stenciling spots until the entire surface is covered. Use a fine-tipped brush to tidy up spots with yellow paint; let dry. Finish with two coats of polyurethane varnish, allowing it to dry between coats.**

TORTOISESHELL FINISH

1 **Paint a box and lid yellow; let dry. Apply a thin layer of transparent glaze to slow the drying time of subsequent paint applications. Using a fine-tipped brush, paint small streaks of sienna. Dot burnt sienna next to raw sienna streaks, all in the same direction.**

2 **Sweep burnt umber over paint smudges. Drag a dry badger brush over the paint to diffuse color. Be sure all paint strokes follow in the same direction. Take care not to cover all of the yellow background.**

3 **Crumple a piece of soft cloth and dab over the entire surface with a light twisting movement. Alternate your hand position and continue dabbing until the mottling appears natural. Finish with two coats of polyurethane varnish, allowing to dry between coats.**

animal-print boxes

An afternoon is all it takes to whip up an attic full of "distressed" do-it-yourself antiques. Here, a special effects paint gives heirloom status to a formerly uninspiring plant stand; the same ultra-easy technique works wonders on old chairs, dressers and mirror frames.

You need: Wooden plant stand; all-purpose primer; Jo Sonja's Acrylic Gouache Colors in burnished copper and titanium white; Jo Sonja crackle medium; waterbased matte finish varnish; #120, #220 and #600 sandpapers; tack cloth; 1"/2.5cm flat paintbrush; 2"/5.1cm flat soft bristle brush; ½"/1.3cm stencil brush; #3 round artist's brush; stencils to fit center top, horizontally around base and vertically along base of plant stand; stencil adhesive; paper plate; paper towels.

Preparing surface: Sand using #120, then #220 sandpapers. Wipe clean with tack cloth. Using 1"/2.5cm brush, apply one to two coats of primer to all surfaces following label directions. Let dry thoroughly. Sand with #220 sandpaper. Wipe clean with tack cloth.

Painting: Using 1"/2.5cm brush, apply two coats of copper, allowing each coat to dry before applying the next coat. Let dry overnight.

Crackling: Using 1"/2.5cm brush, apply four heavy coats of white. Allow each coat to be just dry to touch before applying next. The thicker and fresher the paint the better the crackle effect. Do not apply heat to speed up drying or paint will cure too much to crackle. When final coat is just dry to touch, apply crackle medium as evenly as possible using 2"/5.1cm brush. Crackling will begin immediately. Let dry 24 hours then sand smooth using #600 sandpaper. Wipe clean with tack cloth.

Stenciling: Refer to stenciling how-tos on page 11. Referring to photo, work from the top down, allowing each section to dry before proceeding to the next section. Spray back of each stencil with adhesive and stencil using burnished copper. To stencil around curves, bend stencil slightly without distorting design or raising edges and brush over areas that are flush with surface. Remove stencil, wait for paint to dry and continue until design is completed. When all stenciling is completed, let dry overnight.

Accent painting: Using #3 round brush, outline selected areas as shown. Let dry overnight.

Finishing: Using 1"/2.5cm brush, apply two coats of varnish, allowing each coat to dry before applying next coat. Let dry 24 hours before using.

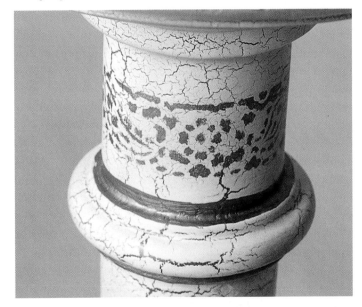

crackled plant stand

Bring a little luxury into your living space. Faux finishing transforms a battered old clock into a prized possession. A careful blend of paints and cunning brushwork mimics the look of malachite on this or any other flat surface in need of a makeover.

You need: Wooden mantle clock; all-purpose primer; acrylic craft paint in white, turquoise and dark green; acrylic craft paint extender; pencil; straight edge; small plastic cups; waterbased satin finish varnish; #120, #220 and #400 sandpapers; tack cloth; 1"/2.5cm flat paintbrush; three ½"/1.3cm flat brushes; blue painter's tape; container lid such as used for cottage cheese; scissors; craft knife; paper towels.

Preparing surface: Remove clock works. Sand clock using #120, then #220 sandpapers. Wipe clean with tack cloth. Using 1"/2.5cm brush, apply two coats of primer following label directions. Let dry thoroughly. Sand with #220 sandpaper. Wipe clean with tack cloth.

Painting: In a cup, mix one part white paint with one part turquoise. Using 1"/ 2.5cm brush, apply two coats, allowing each coat to dry before applying the next coat. Let dry thoroughly. Sand with #400 sand-paper. Wipe clean with tack cloth.

Real malachite is veneered to surfaces in segments. To simulate this look, use pencil and straight edge to lightly mark edges of segments as shown. Use painter's tape to outline as many non-adjacent segments as possible.

Graining: To make graining tools, trim rim from container lid with scissors. Use craft knife and straight edge to cut lid in half. Along each straight edge use scissors to cut notches and teeth in various widths. The more intricate and varied the notches, the more realistic the effect will be; refer to photo. Cut each tool, perpendicular to the edge, into three to four pieces.

Make dark turquoise glaze by mixing one part turquoise in a cup with ¼ part dark green, ¼ part water and ½ part extender. Make white glaze by mixing one part white in a cup with ¼ part water and ½ part extender. Make dark green glaze by mixing one part dark green in a cup with ¼ part water and ½ part extender.

Using ½"/1.3cm brush for each glaze color, glaze one segment at a time. Apply wide bands of dark turquoise next to smaller bands of white and still smaller bands of dark green. Immediately drag graining tools across surface. Use one, two or three tools for each segment, varying direction of graining within segment as shown. Clean edges of tools with paper towels. Let dry two hours and remove tape. Let dry four hours. Tape edges of segments that have not been grained and repeat. Let dry overnight.

Finishing: Using 1"/2.5cm brush, apply two coats of varnish, allowing each coat to dry before applying next coat. Let dry 24 hours before using.

Assembling: Insert clock works.

malachite clock

Perk up the patio or porch with terracotta pots painted with fine lines of zingy color. Vary thickness and the distance between each stripe for visual interest or paint a square motif for a post-modern finish. Fill with your favorite green things and let the sun shine in.

STRIPED FLOWER POTS

You need: Terracotta pots, about 11"H x 12"W/28cm x 30.5cm; exterior paints in white and other colors as desired; exterior varnish; pencil; assorted paintbrushes; tape measure; ruler.

Preparing pots: Paint outside of pot with two coats of white paint, letting dry after each coat. Using tape measure as guide, lightly draw stripes with pencil at random intervals around pot, checking spacing with ruler.

Painting: Using assorted-sized brushes, paint stripes over marked lines, varying width of stripes; let dry.

Finishing: Coat outside of pot with two coats of varnish, letting dry after each coat.

SQUARE-MOTIF POTS

You need: Terra-cotta pots; acrylic paint in white and shades of blue (or desired colors); foam brush; 1"/2.5cm-wide masking tape; spray sealer.

Preparing pots: Paint inside and outside of pot with two to three coats of white acrylic; letting dry between coats. (Painting inside of pots seals terra-cotta and prevents moisture from seeping through and flaking off paint.)

Decorating: Tear off four 3"/7.3cm-long pieces of tape. Adhere to pot to create square shape. Paint outside of pot desired color; be sure that paint does not seep underneath tape. Let paint dry a few moments, then carefully peel off tape. Let dry completely.

Finishing: Spray pot with one to two light coats of sealer, drying between applications.

easy flower pots

WORK BENCH

You need: Wooden work bench; all-purpose primer; indoor/outdoor acrylic semi-gloss paint in red; #120 and #220 sandpapers; tack cloth; 2"/5cm flat paintbrush.

Preparing surface: Sand all surfaces of bench, including undersides, using #120, then #220 sandpapers. Wipe clean with tack cloth. Apply one to two coats of primer to all surfaces following label directions. Let dry thoroughly. Sand with #220 sandpaper. Wipe clean with tack cloth.

Painting: Apply two to three coats of red, allowing each coat to dry before applying next coat. For best results, lightly sand between coats using #220 sandpaper and wipe clean with tack cloth; do not sand after last coat. Let dry 24 hours before using.

BIRDHOUSES

You need: Wooden birdhouses; all-purpose primer; indoor/outdoor acrylic paint in red, white, dark blue and dark gray; #120 and #220 sandpapers; tack cloth; 1"/2.5cm flat paintbrush; artist's brushes: $1/_8$"/3cm, $1/_4$"/.6cm and $1/_2$"/1.3cm flat, and #1 and #3 round.

Preparing surface: Sand all surfaces, including undersides, using #120, then #220 sandpapers. Wipe clean with tack cloth. Using 1"/2.5cm brush, apply one to two coats of primer to all surfaces following label directions. Let dry thoroughly. Sand with #220 sandpaper. Wipe clean with tack cloth.

Painting: Refer to photo for suggested color combinations and details. For each section, apply two to three coats of paint, allowing each coat to dry before applying next coat and using a flat brush size to match size of area being painted. Paint small details like a window frame using $1/_8$"/3cm flat brush and flowers and brushes using #1 and #3 round brushes. Let dry 24 hours before using.

WATERING CANS

You need: Old or new galvanized watering cans; aerosol metal primer; high-gloss aerosol enamel paint in red, white and blue; #220 sandpaper; old sheets or drop cloths.

Preparing watering cans: Sand to remove any loose paint, rust and to rough up surface for better primer adhesion. Wash well to remove dirt and debris. Let dry completely.

Priming: Work in a well ventilated area. Place watering can on sheet or drop cloth, then protect surrounding area to prevent over-spray. Following label directions, apply one to two coats of primer to outside of watering can, allowing first coat to dry before applying the next. Let dry thoroughly.

Painting: Working as for priming, apply two to three coats of enamel following application tips and drying times on label. Let dry 24 hours before using.

Create a bright spot for the garden with galvanized watering cans, buckets and a nifty work bench painted in a cheerful array of vibrant shades. On their own or filled with flowers, they make winsome accents for a table, porch or patio.

painted watering cans, bench and birdhouses

Miniature chests of drawers stacked one atop the other make a handy holding place for bath and beauty items such as barrettes, cotton balls, trial size lotions and the like. Paint in pastel colors, then run a comb through the still-wet paint for a groovy effect.

You need: Two wooden apothecary cabinets with wooden knobs; all-purpose primer; acrylic craft paint in pale olive green, light olive green, medium olive green, light blue, medium blue and medium yellow; waterbased satin finish varnish; screwdriver; #120 and #220 sandpapers; tack cloth; 1"/2.5cm flat paintbrush; ½"/1.3cm flat artist's brush; three 1"/2.5cm disposable sponge brushes (one for each color); paper plates; combing tool; paper towels.

Preparing surface: Remove drawers and knobs. Sand all surfaces to be painted using #120, then #220 sandpapers. Wipe clean with tack cloth. Using 1"/2.5cm brush, apply one coat of primer following label directions. Let dry thoroughly. Sand all surfaces with #220 sandpaper. Wipe clean with tack cloth.

Painting: Using 1"/2.5cm brush, apply two coats of pale olive to all sides of each cabinet and to drawers (omitting fronts), allowing each coat to dry thoroughly before applying the next coat. For best results, lightly sand between coats using #220 sandpaper and wipe clean with tack cloth; do not sand after last coat. Using ½"/1.3cm brush, paint four drawer fronts each using light olive, light blue and medium yellow. Paint knobs using a mix of light olive and medium yellow. Let dry overnight.

Combing: On a paper plate, mix one part medium olive green with one part water to make a glaze. Using foam brush, apply one coat of glaze to light olive green drawer front. Using combing tool, drag comb through wet glaze making horizontal wavy lines. While glaze is still wet, use end of ½"/1.3cm brush to drag four horizontal lines, as shown. Wipe comb clean with paper towel. Make one more in the same manner, then two combing vertical wavy lines. Using medium blue for glaze, comb one light blue drawer front horizontally and three vertically. Using light olive green for glaze for yellow drawer fronts, comb two horizontally and two vertically. Let dry overnight.

Finishing: Apply of two coats of varnish to all surfaces and knobs, allowing each coat to dry before applying next coat. Let dry 24 hours before using. Install knobs, then slide in drawers following photo for placement.

apothecary cabinets

You need: Wooden wall clock with clock insert; all-purpose primer; acrylic craft paint in light turquoise, light green and medium gray; acrylic craft paint extender; paper plates; waterbased matte finish varnish; #120 and #220 sandpapers; tack cloth; 1"/2.5cm and ½"/1.3cm flat paintbrushes; cherry patterned wallpaper; small, sharp scissors; découpage medium; cheese cloth.

Preparing surface: Remove clock insert; set aside. Sand using #120, then #220 sandpapers. Wipe clean with tack cloth. Using 1"/2.5cm brush, apply one to two coats of primer to all surfaces following label directions. Let dry thoroughly. Sand with #220 sandpaper. Wipe clean with tack cloth.

Painting: Using 1"/2.5cm brush, apply two coats of paint, allowing each coat to dry before applying the next coat. Paint front and back of clock light turquoise and edge light green. Let dry thoroughly.

Color-washing: Make medium gray glaze by mixing one part paint with one part water and one part extender. Dip cheese cloth into glaze. Wipe cloth on surface to apply color. Use damp cloth to wipe off excess color as needed. Let dry overnight.

Weathering: Using #220 sandpaper, sand edges down to raw wood as shown. Wipe clean with tack cloth.

Découpage: Cut motifs from wallpaper. Use ½"/1.3cm brush to apply medium to back of motifs. Position on clock and smooth with damp cheese cloth. Let dry overnight.

Finishing: Using 1"/2.5cm brush, apply two coats of varnish, allowing each coat to dry before applying next coat. Let dry 24 hours before using.

Assembling: Install clock insert.

TIP

Using too much medium may cause the paper to tear or prevent it from lying flat so be sure to apply medium lightly and evenly. A foam throw-away brush also comes in handy when working with larger images.

Set aside an hour or so in your busy schedule to try your hand at this charming kitchen timekeeper. A little skill with a brush, pastel paints and artfully-placed clusters of fresh cherries are all it takes to lend an antique look to a plain wood clock.

country clock

The vases displaying these bright blooms and houseplant cuttings started out as old glass bottles and jars. A quick rinse and a few fat brushstrokes of green, blue and yellow paint transform them into a glorious collection of eye-catching vases.

You need: Clear glass bottles, jars, and vases; Liquitex® Glossies™ acrylic enamels in desired colors; ½"/1.3cm-wide Scotch 3M #230 Drafting tape; #6 round artist's paintbrush; disposable plastic plate; paper towels.

Note: Paint is intended for decorative surfaces only.

Preparation: Wash bottles with detergent and warm water. Allow to dry.

Painting: Pour desired color onto plastic plate. Dip brush into paint and brush paint onto glass from the top edge to the bottom. Use even pressure and make one continuous stroke for each stripe. Be sure you have enough paint on the brush to complete the stripe without stopping to reload the brush. With practice you will be able to judge the amount of paint to use for the size of the project you are painting. To vary the width of the stripe, apply more pressure to the brush for a wide strip and less pressure for a narrow stripe.

To ensure that the stripes are absolutely vertical, place the area to be painted directly in front of you. Turn the project after each stripe so the new area to be striped is in front of you. To move the project, place your fingers in the neck of the glass or bottle to avoid touching the painted areas.

ACRYLIC PAINT

Because acrylic paints tend to dry quickly, squeeze out paint a little at a time. If you're using a plastic plate as a palette, keep a spray bottle handy and occassionally, spray the paint with a fine mist to keep it moist. Once you've completed your project, save your unused paint by storing each color in a separate film canister, and dab the paint color on the lid.

striped vases

You need: Wooden trash can shed with wrought iron hardware; 5" x 12"/12.7cm x 30.5 piece of ½"/.6cm-thick exterior grade plywood with one good face for plaque; four 1"/2.5cm-diameter wooden ball knobs; four #10 screws; metal coat hook and screws; all-purpose primer; indoor/outdoor acrylic paint in white, dark green, light and dark yellow, light, medium and dark fuchsia, orange, blue, and green; #120 and #220 sandpapers; tack cloth; 1"/2.5cm and 2"/5cm flat paintbrushes; artist's brushes: ¼"/.6cm and ½"/1.3cm flat, #3 and #6 round; blue painter's tape; 3" self-stick vinyl letters in T, R, A, S and H; 1yd/1m of black nylon cord; screwdriver; power drill; ⅛"/.3cm and ³⁄₁₆"/.4cm drill bits; ruler; pencil; scissors.

Installing hook: On door, measure and mark for hook. Drill pilot holes for screws using ⅛"/.3cm drill bit. Install hook using screws.

Drilling holes in plaque: Measure and mark 1¼"/3cm from top edge and 2½"/6.3cm from side edges. Drill holes using ³⁄₁₆"/.4cm drill bit.

Preparing surface: Remove wrought iron hardware and set aside. Sand all surfaces of shed, including inside, and plaque using #120, then #220 sandpapers. Wipe clean with tack cloth. Using 1"/1.3cm brush for small areas and 2"/5cm bush for large areas, apply two coats of primer to all surfaces, including hook, following label directions. Let dry thoroughly. Sand with #220 sandpaper. Wipe clean with tack cloth.

Painting shed: Use 1"/2.5cm brush for small areas and 2"/5cm bush for large areas. Apply two to three coats of indoor/outdoor acrylic white to shed and hook, allowing each coat to dry thoroughly before applying the next coat. For best results, lightly sand between coats using #220 sandpaper and wipe clean with tack cloth; do not sand after last coat. Let dry overnight. Working in the same manner, use ½"/1.3cm brush to paint edge of roof dark green; let dry.

Painting flowers: Refer to photo for suggested design and color placement. Lightly pencil flower heads, stems and leaves. Use #6 brush for large areas, ¼"/.6cm and #3 brush for medium areas and small details. Allow each color to dry before applying next color. Paint stems first. Paint flower heads second as follows: paint petals main color, highlight petals with lighter color and white, paint centers, then highlight with lighter color. Paint leaves third as follows: paint leaves main color, then highlight with lighter color. Paint grass fourth. After all painting is completed, let dry overnight.

Painting plaque: Use 1"/2.5cm for larger areas and ½"/1.3cm brush for small areas. Working as for shed, apply two to three coats of white to good face (front). Apply two to three coats of dark green to back and side edges. Let dry overnight. Using painter's tape, mask off for a 1"/2.5cm border all around front. Paint border green. Paint ball knobs fuchsia. After all painting is completed, let dry overnight.

Finishing plaque: Use ³⁄₁₆"/.4cm drill bit to drill holes in each corner for ball knobs. Adhere vinyl letters. Install ball knobs using #10 screws. Thread cord through holes at top of plaque.

Assembling: Install hardware and rehang door. Hang plaque, trimming off excess cord.

Paint a container cute for unsightly trash and recycling cans. Slicked with white and edged with a bottom border of blue and purple blooms, it features a hand-lettered sign on the door to indicate contents.

trash can shed

"AT THE BEACH" SIGN

You need: 25"/63.5cm-length of 1" x 7"/2.5cm x 17.5cm clear pine; assorted wooden ornaments; acrylic craft paint in same colors as for "We are" sign (page 126); waterbased satin finish varnish; #120 and #220 sandpapers; tack cloth; pencil; 1"/2.5cm flat paintbrush; artist's brushes: #3 round, ¼"/.6cm and ½"/1.3cm flat; sea sponge; power drill with ⅛"/3mm bit; jute twine; ruler; scissors.

Preparing surface: Sand using #120, then #220 sandpapers. Wipe clean with tack cloth.

Prepping board: Drill two small holes in top and two in bottom as shown. With rag, rub on white paint.

Painting: Sponge-paint random colors. Pencil in narrow border and freehand "at the beach" Paint as desired.

Finishing: Using 1"/2.5cm flat brush, apply two coats of varnish to all pieces, allowing each coat to dry before applying next coat. Let dry 24 hours before using.

Assembling: Cut two 18"L pieces twine. Thread/tie one as hanger; the other, through ornaments and then board. (If needed, drill holes in ornaments first.)

DOOR HANGER SIGN

You need: Wooden paddle; all-purpose primer; acrylic craft paint in color shown or as desired; paint pen in black; waterbased satin finish varnish; #120 and #220 sandpapers; tack cloth; ½"/1.3cm flat artist's brush; jute or hemp twine.

Preparing surface: Sand using #120, then #220 sandpapers. Wipe clean with tack cloth. Apply one coat of primer following label directions. Let dry thoroughly. Sand with #220 sandpaper. Wipe clean with tack cloth.

Painting: Apply two to three coats of paint, allowing each coat to dry before applying next coat. For best results, lightly sand between coats using #220 sandpaper and wipe clean with tack cloth; do not sand after last coat. Let dry overnight.

Lettering: Using paint pen, write desired phrase or message. Let dry.

Finishing: Apply two coats of varnish, allowing each coat to dry before applying next coat. Let dry 24 hours. Attach a loop of twine.

at the beach...

LUNCH

served

at NOON

we are

fishing	
shopping	✔
swimming	
sleeping	

Handpainted signs give weekend guests a warm welcome and let them know where to find the hosts. All make a delightful extra (or great hostess gift) for a beach bungalow or country cottage; follow our examples or custom create a message that works for you.

signs of the times

"WE ARE" SIGN

You need: 12"/30.5cm-length of 1" x 12"/2.5cm x 30.5cm clear pine; 2" x 4"/5cm x 10cm piece of balsa wood for check mark; acrylic craft paint in wicker white, pure orange, light periwinkle, sunny yellow, kelly green, aqua and black; waterbased satin finish varnish; #120 and #220 sandpapers; tack cloth; tracing paper; transfer paper; pencil; cotton rag; 1"/2.5cm flat paintbrush; artist's brushes: #3 and #6 round, ¼"/.6cm and ½"/1.3cm flat; sea sponge; masking tape; craft knife; power drill with ⅛"/3mm bit; wire for hanging; 1⅛"/2.7cm-long white self-adhesive hook and loop fastener.

Preparing surface: Sand using #120, then #220 sandpapers. Wipe clean with tack cloth.

Prepping pine board: Drill two holes where indicated on pattern. With rag, rub on white paint.

Making patterns: Enlarge and copy check mark and sign (feel free to substitute your own favorite activities) onto separate pieces of tracing paper.

Painting: Place sign tracing on wood; slip transfer paper underneath; tape; trace. Draw a 1"/2.5cm grid in background. Sponge-paint chart with aqua, green, yellow, orange. Paint "We are" orange; outline in black. Paint activities in black. Paint grid lines periwinkle.

Making check mark: Trace pattern to balsa wood; cut out with craft knife. Paint aqua. Adhere piece of hook side of fastener to back of check mark.

Finishing: Using 1"/2.5cm flat brush, apply two coats of varnish to all pieces, allowing each coat to dry before applying next coat. Let dry 24 hours before using.

Assembling: Thread wire through holes; twist ends. Cut small pieces of loop side of fastener; adhere to sign at X's.

"We are" sign   1 square = 1"

"LUNCH" SIGN

You need: Clear pine: 16"/40.5cm-length of 1" x 6"/2.5cm x 15.2cm, 10"/25.4cm-length of 1" x 3"/2.5cm x 7.6cm, 8"/20.3cm-length of 1" x 4"/2.5cm x 10cm; acrylic craft paint in wicker white, aqua, magenta, sunny yellow, kelly green, periwinkle and black; waterbased satin finish varnish; #120 and #220 sandpapers; tack cloth; tracing paper; transfer paper; pencil; cotton rag; 1"/2.5cm flat paintbrush; artist's brushes: #3 and #6 round, ¼"/.6cm and ½"/1.3cm flat; checkerboard stencil; ½"/1.3cm stencil brush; sea sponge; masking tape; yardstick; power drill with ⅛"/3mm bit; eight small screw eyes; 8"/20.3cm-length of chain; pliers; sawtooth hanger; hammer.

Preparing surface: Sand using #120, then #220 sandpapers. Wipe clean with tack cloth.

Painting: With rag, rub on white.

Adding lettering: Enlarge patterns for lettering. Position lettering patterns on wood pieces as shown. Slip the transfer paper underneath; tape. Trace.

Painting: Position the checkerboard stencil on wood. Stencil aqua check around lettering. Mix magenta with some white; paint "Lunch" lettering. Add highlights with a lighter shade of magenta (add some more white) and shading with unmixed magenta. When dry, outline lettering with black. "Served", mix kelly green with yellow (lime green); paint wood. When dry, paint lettering in black. "At noon", sponge-paint wood periwinkle. Paint a border around wood with magenta. Add the lettering with black.

Finishing: Using 1"/2.5cm flat brush, apply two coats of varnish to all pieces, allowing each coat to dry before applying next coat. Let dry 24 hours before using.

Drilling holes: Lay all three pieces face up, centering pieces as shown in photo. With a yardstick held vertically across the three pieces (5"/12.7cm in from ends of long top piece) mark placement for drilled holes. Transfer these marks to the bottom edge of top piece, top and bottom of middle piece and top edge of bottom piece. Drill holes.

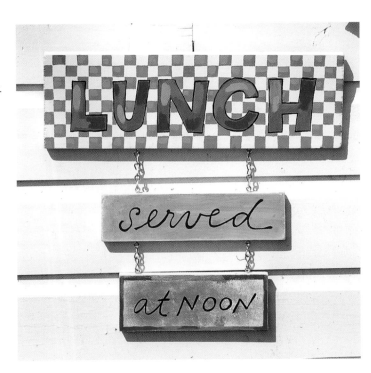

Join pieces with 2"/5cm lengths of chain attached to screw eyes. (Open and close the individual links with pliers.)

Hanging: Attach sawtooth hanger back of "Lunch" piece.

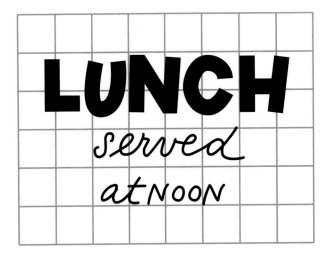

"LUNCH" sign   1 square = 2"

Bold bands of color are the perfect pick-me-up. Bring them into the bath for an eye-opening accent. Use masking tape to mark off stripes on a purchased plain curtain or panel of sheer fabric, then brush on color between the strips of tape.

CURTAINS

You need: Sheer white shower curtains; fabric paints in bright red, deep red and chestnut brown; stencil brush or foam pouncer; paper plates or paint palette; ½"/1.3cm-wide blue painter's tape; large piece of cardboard; paper towels; yardstick; iron.

Preparing curtain: Cover work surface with cardboard. Spread lower edge of curtain over cardboard; tape edges. Starting about 6"/15cm from lower edge of curtain, apply a row of tape. Measure frequently and use yardstick as guide to keep tape straight. Apply additional rows of tape, spaced as desired.

Painting: Pour small amount of paint onto plate. Pounce brush in paint, then on paper towel to remove excess. Pounce paint on curtain, forming stripes. Apply remaining colors of paint in same manner. Let dry.

Heat setting: Use iron to heat-set following paint manufacturer's directions.

TIP

Simple stripes can be far from simple. First time painters often paint too many stripes. Use a brush with long, fine-pointed bristles and draw stripes by gliding brush lightly across.

striped shower curtain

The brighter, the better—perk up the playroom, bedroom or nursery with a splash of painted-on color.

kid stuff

dressers, toy storage and tables and chairs

You need: Child's wooden spindle back rocking chair; 12"/30.5cm square of ½"/ 13mm-thick clear pine; two 1"/ 2.5cm-lengths of ⅜"/10mm-diameter wooden dowel; waterbased satin finish varnish; acrylic craft paint in dark yellow, white, medium blue, black, light red and medium green; black graphite paper; pencil; saber saw; power drill with ⅜"/1cm drill bit; #120 and #220 sandpapers; tack cloth; 1"/2.5cm flat paint brush; artist's brushes: ¼"/.6cm and ½"/1.3cm flat, and #1 and #3 round; 1"/2.5cm-wide blue painter's tape; craft knife; straight edge ruler; cutting mat; wood glue.

Cutting out shapes: Using graphite paper, enlarge and transfer outlines of bird and watermelon slice onto pine. Using saber saw, cut out shapes.

Drilling holes: Referring to photo, position watermelon slice on top of chair crest. Mark for hole in crest and watermelon slice. Drill a ½"/1.3cm-deep hole straight into each mark. Position bird on top of watermelon slice. Mark for hole in bird and watermelon slice; drill holes.

Note: When priming and painting, take care not to get paint into drilled holes.

Preparing surface: Sand all surfaces to be painted using #120, then #220 sandpapers. Wipe clean with tack cloth. Use 1"/2.5cm brush for large areas and ½"/1.3cm brush for small areas. Apply one coat of primer following label directions. Let dry thoroughly. Sand with #220 sandpaper. Wipe clean with tack cloth.

Painting chair: Use ½"/1.3cm brush for small areas and 1"/2.5cm brush for large areas. Apply two coats of yellow to entire chair, allowing each coat to dry thoroughly before applying the next coat. For best results, lightly sand between coats using #220 sandpaper and wipe clean with tack cloth; do not sand after last coat. Let dry overnight. Working in the same manner, apply two coats of white to seat; let dry overnight.

Painting checkerboard seat: Working on cutting mat, cut painter's tape into 1"/2.5cm squares using craft knife and ruler. Adhere first square to center front of seat so ½"/.6cm overlaps onto top of seat and ½"/.6cm overlaps onto front edge. Continue to adhere squares in a checkerboard pattern spacing them 1"/2.5cm apart. Using ¼"/.6cm brush, paint untaped squares blue. Let dry four hours; remove tape. Continue to let dry overnight.

Weathering chair: Using #220 sandpaper, sand random areas down to paint color of layer below or raw wood, as shown. Wipe clean with tack cloth.

Painting bird: Using ½"/1.3cm brush, paint bird blue. Using #3 brush, paint beak yellow. Using #1 brush, paint eyes black. Let dry overnight.

Painting watermelon: Using ¼"/.6cm brush, paint white flesh. Using ½"/1.3cm brush, paint red flesh and rind green. Using #1 brush, paint seeds black. Let dry overnight.

Weathering bird and watermelon: Using #220 sandpaper, sand edges and random areas down to raw wood. Wipe clean with tack cloth.

Finishing: Apply two coats of varnish to all pieces, allowing each coat to dry before applying next coat. Let dry overnight.

Assembling: Wood-glue one dowel into crest, then into watermelon slice. Wood-glue other dowel into watermelon slice, then into bird, as show. Let dry overnight before using.

enlarge templates 200%

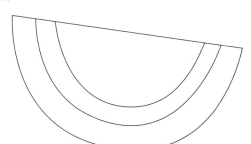

A cool checkerboard pattern and a wash of yellow paint jazz up a child-size rocker. Perfect for the playroom or as a conversation piece almost anywhere else, it provides an inviting spot for little ones (or their stuffed friends) to sit a spell.

rocking chair

Short on space? A table-topped bedside bin provides plenty of storage space and does double duty as an ever-so-hip design element when painted in bold bands of white and blue. Keep it simple as shown or accent with stickers or painted-on motifs.

You need: Wooden bin; ½"/13mm-thick pine board cut ½"/1.3cm larger all around than top of bin for table top; all-purpose primer; acrylic paint in white and blue; waterbased satin finish varnish; #120 and #220 sandpapers; tack cloth; 1"/2.5cm flat paint brush; blue painter's tape; ruler; pencil.

Preparing surface: Sand all surfaces to be painted using #120, then #220 sandpapers. Wipe clean with tack cloth. Apply one to two coats of primer following label directions. Let dry thoroughly. Sand with #220 sandpaper. Wipe clean with tack cloth.

Painting: Apply two to three coats of paint, allowing each coat to dry thoroughly before applying the next coat. For best results, lightly sand between coats using #220 sandpaper and wipe clean with tack cloth; do not sand after last coat. Paint all surfaces white. Let dry overnight.

Painting stripes: Measure height of sides (not including legs), then divide number by 5 to determine width of two blue stripes. Measure and mark for stripe guidelines. Following guidelines, adhere painter's tape slightly below and above each line so lines will be painted over. Paint stripes blue. Let last coat dry two hours, then remove tape. Continue to let dry overnight.

Finishing: Apply two coats of varnish to all surfaces, allowing each coat to dry before applying next coat. Let dry 24 hours before using.

striped bedside bin

Little ones will love being allowed to scribble on this furniture. Chalkboard paint transforms drawer fronts, top and sides into a blank canvas for ever-changing art; use vibrant hues to jazz up the edges.

You need: Wooden dresser with raised panel drawers with 1"/2.5cm-wide frames and wooden knobs; all-purpose primer; Crayola Chalkboard Paint; acrylic craft paints in dark yellow, bright green, cerulean blue and dark orange; waterbased satin finish varnish; #120 and #220 sandpapers; tack cloth; 1"/2.5cm flat paint brush; ½"/1.3cm flat artist's brush; painter's tape; scissors.

Preparing surface: Remove drawers and knobs. Sand all surfaces to be painted (including side and back edges of drawers) and knobs using #120, then #220 sandpapers. Wipe clean with tack cloth. Using 1"/2.5cm brush, apply one to two coats of primer following label directions. Let dry thoroughly. Sand with #220 sandpaper. Wipe clean with tack cloth.

Color painting: Using ½"/1.3cm brush, apply two to three coats of paint to each piece, allowing each coat to dry thoroughly before applying the next coat. For best results, lightly sand between coats using #220 sandpaper and wipe clean with tack cloth; do not sand after last coat. Refer to photo for color placement.

Paint knobs yellow, green and blue. Apply painter's tape along all edges of drawers and dresser where color paint will meet chalkboard paint. Using ½"/1.3cm brush, paint frame, side and back edges of each drawer in colors to correspond to knobs. Paint trim around top and bottom edges of dresser orange. Paint each foot (or leg) a different color.

Let dry overnight.

Finishing: Using ½"/1.3cm brush, apply two coats of varnish to knobs and color trim areas only, allowing each coat to dry before applying next coat. Let dry two hours; remove tape. Continue to let dry overnight.

Chalkboard painting: Apply painter's tape along all edges of drawers and frame where chalkboard paint will meet color paint. Use 1"/2.5cm brush for large areas and ½"/1.3cm brush for tight areas and any needed touch-ups. Apply two to three coats of chalkboard paint following label directions, allowing each coat to dry before applying the next coat. Do not sand between coats. Paint drawer fronts. Paint top, sides and front of dresser. Let dry 24 hours before using.

Assembling: Install knobs, then slide in drawers.

chalkboard dresser

You need: Wooden changing table with wooden knobs; all-purpose primer; indoor/outdoor acrylic paint in white and dark blue; waterbased satin finish varnish; screwdriver; #120 and #220 sandpapers; tack cloth; 1"/2.5cm flat paint brush; blue painter's tape; ruler; pencil; pencil compass; craft knife; 5" x 5"/12.7cm x 12.5cm square of stencil blank; stencil adhesive; small sea sponge; paper plate; paper towels; 2yd/2m of blue and white print fabric; scissors; straight pins; sewing needle; matching sewing thread; sewing machine; iron; 1"/2.5cm-thick foam pad to fit table top; 2yd/2m of self-adhesive hook and loop fastener tape.

Preparing surface: Remove knobs, drawers, door and hardware; set hardware aside. Sand all sides of frame, door, drawers (including side and back edges) and knobs using #120, then #220 sandpapers. Wipe clean with tack cloth. Apply one to two coats of primer following label directions. Let dry thoroughly. Sand with #220 sandpaper. Wipe clean with tack cloth.

Painting: Apply two to three coats of paint, allowing each coat to dry thoroughly before applying the next coat. For best results, lightly sand between coats using #220 sandpaper and wipe clean with tack cloth; do not sand after last coat. Use 1"/2.5cm brush for large areas and ½"/1.3cm brush for tight areas and for any needed touch-ups. Paint table top, door panel and knobs white. Paint all remaining surfaces blue. Let dry overnight.

Stenciling dots: Referring to photo for suggested design and spacing, measure and mark with a small pencil mark, for 1"/2.5cm-diameter dots. Using compass, draw a 1"/2.5cm-diameter circle on stencil blank. Using craft knife, cut out circle. Spray wrong side of stencil with adhesive. Adhere stencil in place, center pencil mark in the middle of the cutout circle. Wet sponge, then wring out until almost dry. Brush blue onto paper plate. Pounce sponge into paint, then pounce onto paper towel to remove excess paint. Lightly pounce onto stencil to apply paint. Lift up stencil and let dry 20 minutes before proceeding to next dot. Clean stencil before repositioning to prevent smudges. Let dry overnight.

Finishing: Apply two coats of varnish to all pieces, allowing each coat to dry before applying next coat. Let dry 24 hours before using.

Assembling: Install hardware, hang door, install knobs, then slide in drawers.

Making pad cover: Cut two pieces of fabric equal to top of pad plus ½"/1.3cm all around for top and bottom of pad cover. Measure perimeter and height of pad; cut one piece of fabric to match dimensions, plus ½"/1.3cm all around for boxing panel. Pin and stitch short ends of boxing panel in ½"/1.3cm seam. Cut two pieces of hook and loop tape, each 3"/7.6cm shorter than pad; separate strips. Adhere, then stitch, loop sections to right side of pad cover bottom, 3"/7.6cm from edges. Pin boxing panel to outer edges of pad cover top and bottom, right sides facing; stitch in ½"/1.3cm seams, leaving opening to insert pad. Turn; insert pad; slipstitch opening closed. Adhere hook sections of fastener strips to changing table.

Paint a plain nursery piece a fun-filled shade and perk up with white and a scattering of sponged-on circles. The changing pad (covered in dotted fabric) attaches with self-adhesive hook and loop strips and can be removed when you are done with diapers.

dotted changing table

Here's a bright idea for stashing playthings. Paint crates in crayon colors, then sponge on circle, moon and star, checkerboard or other fanciful designs for a sprightly touch. Be sure to sand down any rough edges before beginning.

You need: Three wooden crates; all-purpose primer; acrylic paint in yellow, turquoise, dark pink and dark blue; waterbased satin finish varnish; #120 and #220 sandpapers; tack cloth; 1"/2.5cm flat paint brush; ½"/1.3cm flat artist's brush; #120 and #220 sandpapers; tack cloth; four new ½"/1.3cm-thick kitchen sponges; fine tip black permanent marker; scissors; hot glue gun and glue sticks; ruler; four paper plates.

Preparing surface: Sand crates using #120, then #220 sandpapers. Wipe clean with tack cloth. Apply one to two coats of primer following label directions. Let dry thoroughly. Sand with #220 sandpaper. Wipe clean with tack cloth.

Painting: Using 1"/2.5cm brush, apply two to three coats of paint to each crate, allowing each coat to dry thoroughly before applying the next coat. Paint two crates yellow and one crate turquoise. Let dry overnight.

Making stamps: Use one sponge for each stamp. Using marker, draw a 2½"/6.3cm-diameter circle, 3"/7.6-tall star and crescent moon, and a 2"/5cm square. Soak sponges in water to make them easier to cut. Cut out shapes following lines. Cut out four 1" x 1"/2.5cm x 2.5cm squares from leftover sponge for handles. Let dry out. Lay all sponge cut-outs flat; let dry. Hot-glue sponge handles to center back of stamps.

Stamping: Moisten stamping surface with water. Using ½"/1.3cm brush, paint a thin layer of paint on paper plate. Press stamp into paint, then stamp onto crate. Reapply paint for each stamping. Use a separate paper plate for each color.

Refer to photo for suggested designs. Stamp one yellow crate with evenly spaced rows of dark pink circles. Stamp other yellow crate in an overall design with dark blue stars and moons.

Stamp turquoise crate in a checkerboard pattern, using square stamp and yellow. Working one side at a time, position first stamp so top edge of stamp is even with top edge of crate and centered side to side. Stamp squares to the left, spacing them 2"/5cm apart, then stamp to the right in the same manner; let dry. Stamp row below, stamping between the squares of the row above to form the checkerboard pattern; let dry. Continue to work from the top down, allowing each row dry before proceeding to next row. Let dry overnight.

Finishing: Apply two coats of varnish to all pieces, allowing each coat to dry before applying next coat. Let dry 24 hours before using.

stamped toy crates

TOY CHEST

You need: Wooden toy chest; all-purpose primer; Painter's Touch by Rust-Oleum in sun yellow and teal; paint pens in blue and red; #120 and #220 sandpapers; tack cloth; 1"/2.5cm flat paint brush; blue painter's tape; ruler; pencil.

Preparing surface: Sand all surfaces to be painted using #120, then #220 sandpapers. Wipe clean with tack cloth. Apply one to two coats of primer following label directions. Let dry thoroughly. Sand with #220 sandpaper. Wipe clean with tack cloth.

Painting stripes: Apply two to three coats of paint, allowing each coat to dry thoroughly before applying the next coat. For best results, lightly sand between coats using #220 sandpaper and wipe clean with tack cloth; do not sand after last coat. Paint right side of sides and lid and wrong side of lid yellow. Let dry overnight. Measure height of sides, then divide number by three to determine width of center yellow stripe. Measure and mark for top and bottom stripe guidelines. Following guidelines, adhere painter's tape slightly below and above line so lines will be painted over. Paint top and bottom stripes, underside and inside of toy chest teal. Let last coat dry two hours, then remove tape. Continue to let dry overnight.

Referring to photo for color placement, measure depth of lid, then divide number by four to determine widths of yellow stripes. Measure and mark for guidelines on top and underside of lid, extending lines onto side edges. Adhere painter's tape as before. Paint stripes teal. Let last coat dry two hours, then remove tape. Continue to let dry overnight.

Painting details: Using paint pens, draw red X's across each teal stripe, then small and large blue curlicues across each yellow stripe. Let dry 24 hours before using.

TABLE AND CHAIR SET

You need: Children's wooden table and chairs; all-purpose primer; Painter's Touch by Rust-Oleum in apple red, berry pink, brilliant blue, grape and sun yellow; #120 and #220 sandpapers; tack cloth; 1"/2.5cm flat paint brush; ½"/1.3cm and ¼"/.6cm flat artist's brushes; blue painter's tape; ruler; pencil; pencil compass; craft knife; stencil blank; stencil adhesive; ½"/13mm stencil brush.

Preparing surface: Sand all surfaces to be painted using #120, then #220 sandpapers. Wipe clean with tack cloth. Using 1"/2.5cm brush, apply one to two coats of primer following label directions. Let dry thoroughly. Sand with #220 sandpaper. Wipe clean with tack cloth.

Painting: Apply two to three coats of paint, allowing each coat to dry thoroughly before applying the next coat. Use 1"/2.5cm brush for large areas, and ½"/1.3cm and ¼"/.6cm brushes for tight areas. Paint light colors first, then dark; stencil spots last (see directions below). Mask off area not being painted with painter's tape. Refer to photo for suggested color placement. Paint each chair using a different color combination. Let dry overnight.

Stenciling spots: Using compass, draw a 4"/10cm-diameter circle on stencil blank. Using craft knife, cut out circle. Refer to stenciling how-tos on page 11. Spray wrong side of stencil with adhesive. Using stenciling brush, stencil yellow and purple circles to top of table, as shown. Wash and dry stencil and brush after each color. Let dry 24 hours before using.

Wide stripes of teal and yellow add pizzazz to an ordinary toy box and make playtime clean-up more fun. Paint pens are the secret to the curlicue squiggles and x's. Right in keeping with all this whimsy: a table-and-chair set in equally beguiling motifs. Oversized spots and sizzling shades on the set offer an energizing place for kids to work on art and craft projects.

toy chest with table-and-chair set

resources

Aleene's/Duncan Enterprises
5673 E. Shields Avenue
Fresno, CA 93727
(800) 438-6226/ (559)291-4444
www.aleenes.com
www.duncancrafts.com

Crayola/Binney & Smith, Inc.
1100 Church Lane
PO Box 431
Easton, PA 18044-0431
(800) 272-9652
www.crayola.com

Fredrix Artist Canvas
PO Box 646
Lawrenceville, GA 30046
www.fredrixartistcanvas.com

Jo Sonja's/Chroma Inc.
205 Bucky Drive
Lititz, PA 17543
(717) 626-8866
www.josonjas.com

Liquitex
(888) 4ACRYLIC
(888) 422-7954
www.liquitex.com

Minwax
(800) 523-9299
www.minwax.com

Plaid Decorator/FolkArt
(800) 842-4197
www.plaidonline.com

Rust Oleum
11 Hawthorn Parkway
Vernon Hills, IL 60061
(800) 553-8444
www.rust-oleum.com

Scotch/3M
(888) 3M HELPS
(888) 364-3577
www.3M.com

Scratch Art
PO Box 303
11 Robbie Road
Avon, MA 02322
(508) 583-8085
www.scratchart.com

Velcro® Brand
406 Brown Avenue
Manchester, NH 03103
(800) 225-0180
www.velcro.com

photo credits